SLATE FROM CONISTON

A history of the Coniston slate industry

SLATE FROM CONISTON

A history of the Coniston Slate Industry

by Alastair Cameron

Published by
Cumbria Amenity Trust
Mining History Society

First impression 1996
Second impression 2005

Published by
Cumbria Amenity Trust Mining History Society
c/o The Secretary
The Heights
Alston
Cumbria
CA9 3DB

Production and layout by
David Sewart
Bourn
Cambridge

Printed by Goodman Baylis & Son Ltd.
The Trinity Press
London Road
Worcester
WR5 2JH

Cumbria Amenity Trust is a county based industrial history society specialising in the industrial archaeology of mining sites and mining communities throughout the county and further afield. The Society is a registered charity and membership is open to all who have an interest in this subject. The Trust produces regular publications for its members and holds frequent visits to sites of interest in Cumbria and other parts of the British Isles. A number of publications are available to the public including a selection of books and interpretative pamphlets on specific sites. Full details can be obtained by writing to the Secretary.

Front Cover: Early morning light on Coniston Old Man, Coniston's 'slate mountain'.

Rear Cover: Mr George Tarr dispatches a clog of slate from the Horse Crag underground workings, Tilberthwaite, Coniston, April 1995.

CHAPTER INDEX

TECHNICAL

GAZETTEER

APPENDIX

FOREWORD

The author of Slate From Coniston, *Alastair Cameron, was born in Coniston and has had connections with the village ever since. Through his father, Jim Cameron, the well-known rock climber and mountaineer, he developed not only a liking for the sport of rock climbing, but an interest in the Lake District as a whole as well, particularly its mountains and their mineral content.*

He has been in a good position to make an extended study of the history of the Slate Quarrying Industry in the Coniston and Torver fells and it would be hard to find a more capable or knowledgeable person to write this fascinating story.

It is the first time that a history of this local industry has been written and this book will be of interest to present-day residents as well as to visitors. Over the years the Slate Quarries have been a valuable source of employment and many generations of local families have worked in the industry.

Major John W B Hext
Holywath, Coniston
December 1995

The Price of the Fine

LONDON SLATE,

Deliver'd on board at *Penny-bridge* in *Lancaſhire*,
Is Two Pounds One Shilling *per* Ton, neat Weight,

Freight to *Hull* about 18 *s. per* Ton.

The Ton covers about twenty-three Yards ſuperficial, at ſeven Yards to the Rood, is three Roods and two Yards.

The Ton is 20 Hundred, the Hundred 112 Pounds.

Particulars may be had of Mr. *William Rigg*, Slate Merchant, in *Hawkſtead, Lancaſhire.*

Copy of a billboard advertising slate for sale through the le Fleming agent, William Rigg. The date is approximately 1790.

INTRODUCTION

On a warm and sultry day in August 1959 an earth moving machine slowly inched its way up the mountainside above Coniston, the sound of its engine echoing across the surrounding fells. The machine was widening the route of what had been a narrow packhorse track running steeply up the flank of Coniston Old Man. The old track led up to a small rocky outcrop, which was known locally as Brossen Stone.

Here, a hundred years before, the 'old men' had worked an outcrop of light green slate. They had driven a level into the mountainside and discovered a pocket of good slate 'metal'. For several years they had worked the slate as an underground chamber or 'closehead'. Eventually they had abandoned it; no doubt the exposed location and difficult access were largely responsible.

It didn't take long to finish the new road up to Brossen. Most of the manpower to complete the work had been drawn from the nearby Old Man Quarries; they were used to working on the mountain, and the August weather had been kind to them. Before the month was out the Old Man face was to echo to the roar of explosives and the growl of engines. Vegetation and peat were removed to the bed-rock. The old level was exposed and cleared out. Brossen Stone quarry was being re-opened.

For Coniston, the development of Brossen by Lakeland Green Slate and Stone Company was to prove to be vital for the future prosperity of the community. The previous year the railway to Coniston had closed with the loss of several jobs. The following year the extensive Old Man Quarries ceased to operate. Had Brossen Stone not re-opened, the overall loss of employment would have been very severe. As it was, the venture was successful. The quarry was developed in a big way. Within ten years it supported around thirty local families and, clearly, it would have a prosperous future.

Brossen Stone is just one of many workings around Coniston which have provided employment for the community for several hundred years. Slate quarrying is extremely skilled and these skills have been passed down through generations of Coniston families. It is an inheritance that has helped give the village its independent character and strong community spirit which is very noticeable today. So long as there is slate to be quarried and worked, and the skills are there to do so, the community spirit will survive. Coniston will never need to rely entirely on tourism for a livelihood.

Coniston is a village with a very strong industrial heritage. Centuries ago, long before the birth of the 'industrial revolution', the woods and lake shores were alive with local industry making use of cheap water power. Slate was not the only

1

material to be taken from the hills. The first records of copper being mined at Coniston are from the 1590s, But there is every possibility that bronze-age man was aware of the outcrops of the veins of copper and made use of them. At the height of activity the Coniston Copper Mine was one of the largest in Europe. The slate industry also became extensive during the 19th Century. We will never know when slate was first extracted, but there is evidence that Roman buildings in the locality made use of Coniston slate.

During the past few decades the market for slate has changed dramatically. Now only a small proportion of the output of the quarries is roofing slate. Because of its properties, slate has found a ready market for architectural work. Many prestigious buildings on all continents are now clad in Coniston slate. As long as architects require a durable material with a beautiful finish there will always be a market for it.

So, a material that was extracted by the Romans is still being worked today. Unfortunately, despite the industry's antiquity, there is hardly any historic reference to it. The chronicles of the Coniston slate industry have never been documented. In fact, very little has been published about it at all. It seemed that a book was crying out to be written. It has taken several years but it has certainly been worth it. Many Coniston people have contributed to it. It has been a true community project. The author makes no apologies for the fact that, at times, he has strayed from the topic of 'slate' to one of the village in general. He does not perceive this as a problem. The history of the industry is inseparable from the history of the village, write about one and you write about the other as well. The culture and personality of the village is as unique as the volcanic slate extracted from its hills.

Much of the historic data has been gleaned from the archives. Data from more recent times has been obtained from conversations with Coniston folk, most of whom have past connections with the industry. Other references have been obtained from more obscure sources, old letters, long forgotten photographs, old newspaper cuttings. It has to be admitted that some assumptions have had to be made. In most cases these are 'calculated guesses' which, hopefully, are close to reality. Far from being a definitive work it is hoped that this book will form the basis for more research so that, in conjunction with existing books and articles on the copper industry, a complete picture of this unusual community can be built up.

THE EARLY YEARS

Coniston slate is 450 million years old. It was formed during the Ordovician era from volcanic ash and dust. It can be split or cleaved into sheets a few millimeters thick and it has great resistance to climatic conditions. As with slate from other parts of Lakeland, it is inert to virtually every form of chemical attack and is considered to be much superior to slate from elsewhere in Europe. As well as the traditional use for roofing, it can also be polished to give a beautiful finish and has become one of the most prized decorative building materials available.

It is impossible to say when quarrying for slate first took place. There is always the possibility that it could have begun in prehistoric times. Early man, as he wandered the high ground in Lakeland, would have been aware of the sites where slate 'outcropped' to the surface. It is quite likely that he would have known of the special qualities of this rather unusual rock.

The Romans in particular would have been aware of the properties of slate. It occurs in several other localities in the former Roman empire, and they probably brought their skills to 'work' slate over with them. But there is hardly any actual evidence surviving of a Roman slate industry although historians report that the Roman fort at Watercrook was roofed in slate and a slate gravestone of Roman origin has been found recently in Ambleside.

Although there is evidence that quarrying for slate was being carried out during these ancient times, it was not until the middle ages that we have anything other than the scantiest of records to show us what was going on. We can only make a calculated guess as to how the early years of the industry developed.

We believe that when the Romans departed, early in the 5th Century, the skills probably departed with them. But by the year 1200 the skills had obviously returned, and the industry was very much alive. What happened in between can only be speculation. It is probable that, for a period of about 600 years, the Saxons made little use of slate. Effectively a 'slate industry' didn't exist in Lakeland at this time although there is some evidence that rough hewn blocks may have been used locally for field walls or even buildings.

It is very likely that the re-birth of the Lakeland slate industry occurred shortly after the Norman Conquest and was caused by the demand for slate to roof monasteries, priories and abbeys as they sprang up across Norman Britain. To the indigenous inhabitants the buildings constructed by their invaders must have appeared startling when compared to their small wooden hovels. It was a complete revolution in building techniques for them. All of the expertise required to build these huge structures in stone would have had to be imported from France and it is very likely that this would have included the working of slate.

Coniston Old Hall, on the shore of Coniston Lake, was the seat of the le Flemings, the Lords of the Manor of Coniston. The present building was much enlarged in 1580 and was last used as the family seat in 1653. The le Flemings kept tight control on the operation of the quarries through an agent until, in 1832, Lady le Fleming decided that she would sell all the leases to the quarries and allow the lease holders the opportunity to operate as they felt best. Today Coniston Old Hall is under the control of the National Trust and, nearby, is the headquarters of the Coniston Sailing Club.   *Photo – A Cameron*

4

We have some evidence to back this up. We know that Calder Abbey, which was founded in 1134, was roofed in green slate. In the south of England, in 1314, slate from the Delabole Quarries in Cornwall was used to repair the roof of Winchester Cathedral. This suggests that the original, damaged, roof was already slated. These two isolated facts, from locations a long way apart, are interesting and tend to suggest that skilled men might have been available to work slate over the entire length of the country during this time.

There is some suggestion, therefore, that the working of slate as we know it today is derived from the Norman invasion. It is interesting to speculate that the techniques used by Coniston quarrymen even in recent times may have originated from skills brought over by Belgian or French artisans with the Conqueror.

There are a number of clues which confirm that this may have occurred. In the great slate mines in the Loire area of France a strange implement known as a 'pioche' was being used to rive slates as far back as the turn of the first millennium. An identical tool has been used in Lakeland slate workings for hundreds of years and is known as a riving hammer. The hammer head consists of a flat sharpened blade on one side and a much narrower sharpened spike on the other. It is very likely that the Lakeland riving hammer has originated from the continent. Riving hammers were used at Coniston right up to the 20th Century, but were eventually replaced by the hammer and chisel.

Other possible links with the ancient French slate industry are also evident. The word 'slate' is derived from the Old French word 'esclate'. Also the rather unusual 'Company' structure which was practically universal in British slate workings was also used extensively in France and Belgium. In the Anjou Valley in the Loire, in Brittany and also the Basson d'Herbeument in Belgium, quarrymen worked in companies or 'societies', setting a 'bargain' for work with quarry owners. At Coniston the Company system worked right up to the 1940s in some quarries.

It is impossible to say exactly where Lakeland slate was first worked. The industry would have developed slowly during the first few hundred years after the Conquest. There is one isolated reference to slate being worked at Sadgill in 1283, but nothing else. As frequently happens in industrial archaeology, historians have to admit defeat and we need to go forward by another three hundred years to be able to continue with the story with any degree of accuracy.

If one was forced to hazard a guess one could do a lot worse than to say that the first areas to be worked for slate after the Norman Conquest in the Coniston area were the high quarries on Coniston Old Man and Brown Pike. Here the presence of slate rock is very evident. It outcrops to the surface and presents itself as natural riven beds. On the high slopes of the Old Man, just below the summit of the mountain, the author has found several places where there is evidence that slate may have been worked by primitive means in these ancient times.

At a much later date, during the sixteenth century the communities of the South Lakeland valleys saw major changes taking place. It all occurred as a result of the dissolution of the monasteries. In 1537 Furness Abbey was 'dissolved' and many of the other ecclesiastical houses in the area were affected at the same time, the last being Cartmel Priory in 1540. Furness Abbey held vast areas of land. This now fell into secular hands and, as a result, there was a major re-casting of the local economy. The local industries such as bloomery hearths, charcoal burning and slate working continued to operate but the trade was no longer organised by and centred round the monasteries and tended to be drawn to the market towns on the fringes of the Lake District. Prior to 1537 a proportion of the land round Torver and Coniston was controlled by the Abbey who set up the local settlements, or 'grounds'. One must assume the slate quarries on the fells would also come under their control as well. These were interesting times but, unfortunately, few records survive.

Although some records exist of the transport of slate from Coniston from as far back as the 1650s, it is not until the 1680s that we have any firm details of the slate industry itself on the Coniston Fells. By this time quarrying in our area was well established. The Tilberthwaite, Old Man and Walna Scar quarries were active and labour was well organised. Records from the period show that slate was being mined as well as quarried. In 1693 Michael Nolan of Hawkshead was killed above Coniston when "bursting a crag". The Coniston Parish Registers also record specific details of a number of slaters residing within the parish including Christopher Nicholson in November 1689 and William Rowenson in January 1693. In 1688 old records show that slate was being exported from Piel Harbour in Low Furness.

Future work in archives and church records may reveal more details of the slate industry between the Norman Conquest and the sixteen hundreds. The le Fleming archives in the County Record Office in Kendal contain un-researched information from this time, much of which is in French and Latin. Until this data is evaluated we can only rely on calculated guesses.

Named after the quarryman who was skilled at constructing such tunnels, a Matty Spedding level runs beneath the tip at Parrock Quarry, Tilberthwaite. Matty worked in the Tilberthwaite area in the first half of the 19th Century and there are many examples of this type of tunnelling around. The sides were built of slate waste which was cantilevered for rigidity and then slabs placed over to form a roof. Despite the rough appearance, Mat Spedding tunnels were extremely safe and allowed quarrymen secure access through unstable ground or through an area which was being worked above.

It is interesting to note that in slate workings in the Ardennes area of Belgium there are tunnels of exactly the same construction. We believe that many of the slate working techniques used in Britain were derived from those used in Belgium and France and were 'imported' shortly after the Norman Conquest.

Photo – A Cameron

THE 18th CENTURY

By the 1770s a healthy and extensive industry was operating in High Furness based on Coniston Old Man and surrounding fells, with most of the major quarries – Gold Scope, Cove, Scald Cop and Saddlestone – in production and, because of their size, most of these must have been working for at least 200 years.

We know that by 1720 the sedimentary slates of Monk Coniston Tarn were being worked extensively by the Swainsons. Product from these workings in the woods above the head of Coniston Lake was used extensively round the Furness area including for the roofing of Ulverston parish church. Many of the dozens of small workings on the fells and in the woods round Coniston would also be working at this time, although perhaps not continually.

But the big quarries, the important quarries, were high on the Old Man and Walna Scar. They exploited the excellent 'metal' of the silver-grey band. It is not known which one has the claim for greatest antiquity, though Scald Cop on the Old Man is very old, judging from the tunnel in the extremity of the lowest closehead which is far too restrictive to allow bogeys to pass and is scarcely wider than a coffin level. On the other side of the mountain, on the slopes of Brown Pike, the Gold Scope workings are also ancient. The name is identical to that of the Elizabethan copper mine near Keswick which has its origins in the German 'Gottes Gab' or 'God's Gift'. German miners were involved in establishing both the Keswick and Coniston copper workings but there is no indication that they were in any way associated with the slate industry.

Although the historian has little tangible information as to how and when these early quarries started, there is much more data available of the transport of finished slate away from Coniston to the customer. In 1688 Coniston slate was being exported from Piel Harbour on the Furness coast. The journey to Piel was by boat along Coniston Lake and then by cart through Low Furness. This method of transport continued right through the 1700s. Later a small port was established at Penny Bridge right at the head of the Crake estuary. The area of land where the port was sited frequently silted up and was replaced by more modern facilities at Greenodd slightly down-stream. In 1772 it is estimated that some 2000 tons of slate was transported to Greenodd from Coniston. Slate would be brought down from the quarries by cart and loaded onto boats at Kirkby Quay near the head of the Lake. There is some suggestion that boats would continue past the foot of the Lake and off-load into carts at Allen Tarn, a short distance down the River Crake. There is a considerable amount of slate lying in the bed of the river at this point. Greenodd became a thriving little port, one of the busiest on this stretch of coast.

Here the slate would be trans-shipped again from the carts into the holds of coastal sloops that would carry the slate to ports round the coast of Britain and Ireland.

When one considers the various stages in the transport of slate from the quarry to the expanding industrial towns, it is not surprising that the cost of transport formed a significant portion of the overall cost to the end user. But if you lived near to the source, and could collect the material yourself, the cost was well within the pocket of many, not just the wealthy land-owning families and religious houses. Thus, by the 1750s, many farms and even small dwellings in South Lakeland had the luxury of being roofed in slate and in 1779 West wrote, "*all Coniston houses were covered with blue slates.*" No doubt it was not just the roofs but also walls as well and the floors of many dwellings would have been laid with slate flags from one of the local flag quarries. By this time many of the slate and flag quarries at Tilberthwaite, Walna Scar, Torver and Coniston were working continually.

At that time the le Flemings were the lords of the manor. The family had a long and noble history. Richard le Fleming inherited the manor of Thurston, and other lands, by marrying the grand-daughter of the Baron of Urswick in about 1240. The family seat was established on the shore of the 'Thurston Water' at the location now known as Coniston Old Hall. The original dwelling must have been relatively small because, many years later, during the reign of Elizabeth the First, William le Fleming greatly enlarged the premises at huge expense. The enormous cost of this venture, plus the fact that he lived extravagantly, meant that on his death in 1597 the family wealth had been greatly reduced. His widow, Agnes, survived him by over 30 years. She was an exceptional person with great foresight and repurchased much of the estate that had been disposed of. Subsequently, during the Civil War, the resourceful Sir Daniel Fleming moved the family seat to Rydal Hall. For the next thirty years Coniston Hall was occupied by an assortment of relations until, in 1653, the last one died and since then none of the family has returned to live at Coniston.

The lavish lifestyle of a nobleman was not cheap. It was important to retain a steady income from their lands. It was very fortunate for the le Fleming family that there existed on otherwise barren and unproductive upland, rich deposits of copper and slate which provided them with considerable revenue. Understandably they kept a close eye on the slate operations and up to the middle years of the 17th Century they actually operated the Tilberthwaite and Old Man quarries themselves, paying wages to the quarrymen and also those involved in boatage and cartage to Greenodd.

On 13th October 1750 a lease was signed between Sir William le Fleming, grandson of Sir Daniel, and William Rigg of Hawkshead. The lease gave Rigg, and subsequently his son, the permission to work all quarries within the Manor of Coniston. Effectively it put the two in a form of partnership which would last for

A copy of a painting by watercolour artist John 'Warwick' Smith (1749 – 1831) titled 'Loading Slate, Lake Coniston'. We feel that this is a fairly accurate depiction of a slate boat about to set off for the journey to the foot of the lake, with a second boat in tow.

Coniston Lake was an essential highway and at any one time there would have been several boats on the lake. As well as slate, lake-transport included copper ore from the Coniston Mine, charcoal and haematite for the various bloomery sites and also for the Coniston Iron Forge after it opened in 1677. The lake also provided transport for all the general requirements of the village community.

Lake transport declined slightly with the extension of the Lancaster Canal to Kendal in 1819 and was phased out completely after the railway to Coniston opened in June 1859.

Print provided by Peter Fleming

about fifty years. The le Fleming lands included the workings on the Old Man and Walna Scar, Banniside Quarries at Tranearth and several of the Tilberthwaite workings. For some reason the Gold Scope Quarry on Brown Pike did not fall on their lands. Quarries on Broughton Moor were on the Broughton Tower Estate, those at Hodge Close and Brathay were on the Duke of Buccleuch lands while those above Tilberthwaite Ghyll and in Little Langdale were under the control of the Muncaster Estates.

At least once every two years the le Flemings ordered an inventory to be carried out of slate stocks and also equipment and tools in use at the quarries. When one considers that this was well over two hundred years ago, the thoroughness of the inventories is remarkable and virtually identical to those carried out routinely by manufacturing industry today. On the particular day of the stock-take, no stock was allowed to move and no slates were made. William Rigg ordered slates to be counted at each location and the outstanding debts owed on that particular day were also listed. Records of the inventories survive and make interesting reading. One carried out on 21st January 1752 listed slates stocked at Tilberthwaite, Old Man and Penny Rigg quarries, and also at the head of the lake. At the foot of the lake stocks were counted at both Nibthwaite Barn and at Allen Tarn and also at the wharf at Greenodd. By 1752 the le Flemings were also associated with the Walna Scar Quarries and the inventory included stock held here and also at the point of shipment at Duddon Sands.

The value of the stock is also interesting. The stocks of 'London' quality slates at the quarry were valued at 1s-7d per 'load'. At Kirkby Quay the value had increased to 1s-11d. The cost of carting was responsible for this 4 pence increase. At Nibthwaite at the foot of the lake the value had only increased by 1d. but by the time the slate had reached the port of Greenodd the value was now 2s-4d.

It is difficult to imagine, today, the activity on Coniston Lake during this period. As well as slate, a considerable quantity of copper ore was also being carried as well as charcoal and iron ore for the nearby bloomery sites. A thriving industry was created which would continue until the Furness Railway's branch to Coniston opened in 1859. For many years during the 1750s, three boatmen were constantly employed carrying slate. They were Adam Fleming, William Kirkby and Robert Kendal. Of the three, Adam Fleming appeared to carry considerably more than either of the others, judging by the records of payments made to him for 'boatage'. During the same period five carters were paid for bringing slate down from the quarries to the head of the lake and at least six carters were employed to carry slate from the foot of the lake to Greenodd.

Another point of shipment which was used extensively for many years was at Angerton on the Duddon Estuary. This handled slate from Walna Scar Quarry, which is one of the earliest in the district. Slate was carted from there direct to the port, a journey of some ten miles. Much of the route can be traced today. By the end of the 1700s Walna Scar Quarries were already very extensive and it is probably safe to assume that both quarry and port were in use for at least one hundred years previously.

The Lords of the Manor were also keen to make sure that the slate production sites were being operated as efficiently as possible and in June 1792 Lady le Fleming, commissioned John Wilson to carry out a survey of the various working quarries within the manor. It is likely that she was concerned that some workings were not providing anticipated returns. The report gives an interesting reference into the situation at the end of the 1700s.

Wilson stated that the slate deposits at Old (Middle) Cove and High Cove were 'fine' and Low Cove was 'superfine'. These quarries, which were both open and underground, are situated on the south west flank of the Old Man in a deep combe also known as The Cove. At that time Low Cove employed ten men but was felt by Wilson to require more investment to achieve its full potential. In particular, another level should be driven to intersect the silver-grey slate band. The middle quarry at Cove was 'rubbished up' and needed 'putting in order'. The quarry floor was swamped with waste slate and debris from the overshadowing crag. There was little room to work the face and the floor would require 'mucking out' which would involve time, labour and capital. The same comments were made of High Cove although this section of the quarry had only started to be developed.

John Wilson's survey was not confined to Cove. He also reported on the Saddlestone workings on the north east shoulder of the mountain. At that time in the 1790s, Saddlestone employed five men and it was also 'rubbished up', showing 'middling' prospects and needing another level driving into the silver-grey band. Above Saddlestone, the workings at Scald Cop were in a similar state but, he felt, would be worthy of further investment. Below Saddlestone the Brandy Crag closehead, which couldn't have been much smaller than it is today, possessed fine reserves and had 'extraordinary prospects'.

Across the Mines Valley the survey reported on the Lad Stone End quarry. This, Wilson felt, had very good prospects and contained a large quantity of slate metal. Despite this though, little further development was to be done at Lad Stone End because it interfered with the expansion of the copper workings on the Bonsor Vein which outcropped nearby.

It is difficult to say how many of John Wilson's recommendations were ever put into practice. His comments on the Saddlestone workings were heeded, however, and a new development was soon to be started at Moss Head, between Saddlestone and Scald Cop. This was to become one of the largest underground slate workings in England and continued in production until the Old Man quarries closed in the 1950s.

It was not until the late 1700s that proprietors began to negotiate leases with the le Flemings. One such example was in May 1791 when three local men took out a lease on workings at Hall Garth, Tilberthwaite. They were Roger Atkinson of Blawith, Isaac Pritt of Broughton and William Watson of Langdale. The three agreed to sell to Thomas Rigg, son of William, all the slate that was obtained at Hall Garth for a period of seven years. A month later they signed an agreement with Anthony Rollinshaw, a local quarryman, for him and his 'Company' to actually do the work, to operate Hall Garth in a *"workmanlike manner, drive forward the quarry, not to undercut the metal and keep the floor clear of rubbish."*

In 1796 the Ulverston Canal was opened linking the town with the coast. It was only short in length, but it was incredibly useful to the expanding slate industry of Furness. Although more of use to the Gawthwaite quarries it still took away some of the trade that passed through Greenodd from Coniston. But Greenodd continued to flourish. As well as slate, money was to be made from handling cargoes of wood, charcoal, iron and copper ore.

The last years of the 18th Century saw difficult times falling on the industry. This was not a result of over-capacity or competition, but because of a tax levied by the government on coastal shipping. The tax amounted to 10s a ton and the revenue was required to help fund the Napoleonic War. This impost hit the slate merchants at Coniston and Kirkby very hard. It was equivalent to a tax of 20% on value and meant that the merchants could no longer compete with their Welsh counterparts. Parliament was petitioned, to no avail. In less than two years fifty percent of employees at the quarries had been dismissed and huge quantities of slates remained unsold, stock-piled on the quarry banks, in various fields round Coniston village and at the wharves at Coniston Lake, Allen Tarn and Greenodd.

This hit the community of Coniston particularly hard. Eventually, on a day in April 1800, the quarrymen from Tilberthwaite and Coniston gathered together and decided to march to Ulverston in protest. On the way they were joined by others from Torver and Walna Scar. At Lowick quarrymen from Gawthwaite and Kirkby joined them as well. A large 'organised rabble' arrived in Ulverston. They raided warehouses, distributed food amongst themselves in a 'most organised way' and then returned to their homes. The booty would not have lasted for long. It was to be many years before the tax was repealed and good times returned to the village.

As the 1700s came to a close many would be wondering if the new century could possibly bring any signs of new fortunes and better prospects.

This photograph of the Hodge Close pit was taken in about 1910 and shows much of the depth of the quarry at that time. Today the pit is flooded and the water level reaches the base of the dark cave opening on the right.   *Photo – Mrs P Rawes*

THE NINETEENTH CENTURY

The century's turn brought little relief to the impoverished community of Coniston. The two main sources of wealth and employment were at rock bottom. The Coniston Copper Mine was more or less at a standstill. A small quantity of ore was being raised but it would be another 25 years before the great John Taylor, mining engineer and entrepreneur, started to inject momentum into the mines. The slate industry was still running at well below its 1790 production levels. Although the Ulverston Canal had opened in 1796, this had little effect on transport costs. It was just an alternative route for cargo to the coast, and the crippling government tax on coastal shipping was to remain for another thirty years. Transport of material had always been one of Coniston's main problems and would remain so until the Coniston branch of the Furness Railway arrived in the village in 1859.

Other problems would not help the general malaise. Sir Michael le Fleming and the Rigg family were to part company in 1801 with Thomas Rigg moving to become slate agent for Lord Cavendish at Kirkby. We have already seen that, in 1750, the Riggs had been the appointed slate merchants to the le Flemings and the family had been very closely associated with the lords of the manor. In fact Sir Daniel le Fleming had referred to William Rigg as his co-partner when the post of agent had been established. All quarry operations came under the Riggs' watchful eye. They collected annual rents for quarries, royalties for the tons of slate produced and chartered coastal vessels for the dispatch of slate. But now the ties were to be broken.

It is not clear why the le Flemings and Thomas Rigg parted company. We know that the Riggs were unhappy about the low level of royalties that the le Flemings were charging the Coniston quarrymen for each ton of slate. Down at Kirkby Lord Cavendish was charging four times as much. Their departure may have been a setback to the industry for a short time but in the longer term it opened up opportunities for new companies with modern ideas to be started. They would be able to control their own operation rather than have it organised by the Lord of the Manor and his agent. Before too many years had passed two new companies, the Coniston Slate Company and the Mandall Company would start to expand rapidly.

So how extensive were the actual quarrying sites at the turn of the century? Many of the large workings that exist today were already well established. On the fells above Torver the Ash Gill Quarries were already large, but only small workings existed at Tranearth and on Broughton Moor. High up in the mountains the Gold Scope and the lower quarries at Cove were also extensive and on the north east shoulder of Coniston Old Man the Old Man Quarries were in full production. The high workings above Low Water, just below the summit of the mountain were employing ten men and producing healthy quantities of silver-grey slate. But the most extensive workings of all at this time were in the Tilberthwaite Valley where the Penny Rigg, Moss Rigg, Sty Rigg and Little Langdale quarries had been in production for at least 100 years.

At this time many of these operations, both in the wooded valley of Tilberthwaite and on the high fells, were being worked as underground closeheads. In some cases extraction this way continued until the quarry was abandoned. An example of this is at the Old Man Quarries where slate was extracted from underground chambers right up to closure during the 1950s. At other quarries, e.g. Cove and in the Tilberthwaite Valley, the closehead was eventually opened out by removing the chamber roof to form an open pit. In the early years of the industry underground quarrying of slate was a technique peculiar to Lakeland. In 1812 two experienced quarrymen, William Turner and Thomas Casson, left Walna Scar Quarry and 'emigrated' to North Wales. They worked two slate quarries above the Conway Valley by closehead. This was the first Welsh slate to be worked underground and, in doing so, they introduced the technique into the Welsh slate industry. William Casson then went on to operate the Diffwys Casson workings at Blaenau Ffestiniog.

Around 1820 a new development took place at the Old Man Quarries. Two long tunnels of about 200ft each were driven in from the surface to intersect the slate band. The location was between the Saddlestone and Scald Cop workings and this development was very significant because it was the first time that underground quarries had been worked from tunnels of such a length. Prior to this development the adits driven in the Coniston area had been generally short and driven through weathered slate rock. The new quarry was called Moss Head and the opening of it was a bold step considering the barely workable conditions and poor financial returns at that time of the adjacent workings.

In 1819 Coniston's slate industry saw a further slight improvement in fortunes with the opening of the Lancaster Canal on 18th June. This new inland waterway linked Kendal with Lancashire and allowed considerable transport economies when compared to coastal shipping. There was little difference in cost between carting from Coniston to Kendal and carting/boating from Coniston to Greenodd. On the other hand the savings made by avoiding coastal shipping tax were significant. Soon carts loaded with slate were leaving Coniston and trundling over the fells to Kendal and the canal terminus. However, from figures for 'boatage costs' on Coniston Lake, it is quite clear that some slate was still carried by the old route despite the new facility.

In 1824 a Mr Baines, a contemporary writer, commented that, "*the most considerable slate mines in the kingdom are in the Furness Fells. Slate is carried to the estuaries of both the Leven and Duddon, and thence shipped to various ports in the United Kingdom at a rate of about 300 tons weekly. The green slate of Coniston is frequently forwarded to Kendal, and thence by the Lancaster Canal, and other inland navigations with which it is connected, not only into South Lancashire and Yorkshire, but also into the Midlands and southern counties."*

It was quite clear that Mr Baines was impressed with what he saw. but his 'considerable slate mines' would have included the massive and vastly superior Kirkby Quarries who exported their products from the hamlet of Sandside on the Duddon Estuary. He was also quite clearly not the well travelled man he would like to have one believe. The 'most considerable slate mines in the Kingdom' were not located in the Furness Fells but in the sedimentary beds of Snowdonia where, in 1824, Mr Richard Pennant was employing over 900 men in the Penrhyn Quarries alone, a figure far in excess of the total number of quarrymen in the whole of Furness, including Kirkby. A much more enlightened and accurate account of the industry was to appear the following year. *A History of Lancashire* by Mr J Corry was published in 1825. Mr Corry spent some time in the High Furness area, which was then part of Lancashire, researching for his book. He wrote of Coniston, *"The manor of Coniston, though comparatively sterile and unfit for cultivation, especially near its northern boundary, is rich in fossils. The Coniston Fells contain mines of copper ore, which were discovered many years ago.............But the most profitable and abundant fossil production of nature found in the Coniston Fells is excellent slate. In the lofty hills near the head of Coniston Lake, there are several quarries of fine blue slate."*

This photograph was taken at the base of the Hodge Close quarry pit and shows lads clearing rubbish from the quarry floor. Note the hanging points on the side of the tubs, used when the tub was lifted from the quarry floor by the blondin crane.   Photo – Mrs P Rawes

He describes in detail the Tilberthwaite workings. "*At Penny Rigg quarry the slate is conveyed on trucks through a level drain into the side of the rock, at some height above the bottom of the pit.*" He then goes on to detail the quarries belonging to Messrs Woodburn and Coward. These included Close Hill where ten men (probably two Companies of five) were producing ten tons of slate a week and were using one powder barrel every month in doing so, and also Sty Rigg and Moss Rigg. "*As these quarries are not in a 'manor', the liberty of working them is paid for to the township of Tilberthwaite at the rate from £100 to £150 per annum.*" Other quarries mentioned by Mr Corry were Wood and Woodeast Quarries owned by Mr Atkinson, Betsy Crag "*which is the property of Mr Turner and is wrought by running a level under the hill*", and Hodge Close owned by a Mr Parker.

Exactly how the 'township of Tilberthwaite' received the royalty payment, or what they did with the money, has to be left to our imagination. Clearly this was much more beneficial to the community than to pay it to a lord of the manor who would then probably squander much of it on extravagant living.

The report allows us some insight into the Tilberthwaite area at the start of the 1800s. Much of the lower ground was of birch and oak, some having been cleared for pasture. On the west side of the valley six quarries were working and on the east only one (Hodge Close). Virtually all the slate extraction in this area was from underground closeheads and the only surface signs were the banks of spoil which spilled down through the woodland, and the dressing sheds in which the rivers and dressers worked. Somewhere in the region of fifty quarrymen would be working here. The tapping of their riving hammers and the clatter of the rid as it was tipped over the edge of the banks would echo through the trees. High above Penny Rigg, higher than the deep cleft of Tilberthwaite Gill, the Tilberthwaite Copper Mine was in production employing several dozen more. Laden carts of slate and copper ore trundled down the valley road at regular intervals to the head of the lake and at the end of the working day there would be a general exodus from the valley, back to the lodgings on the farms or in the village. For a few hours Tilberthwaite would be peaceful.

At long last, in 1830, the tax on coastal shipping was abolished. This heralded a rapid expansion of the industry nation-wide which, in effect, created a mini boom which would last for forty years. Existing workings which showed good prospects were enlarged and new sites were commenced. In 1832 Lady le Fleming put the leases of the slate quarries up for sale. Records in the le Fleming archives paint an interesting picture. The estate had held onto some control of the quarries after the departure of the Riggs. Despite advice to the contrary Lady le Fleming was quite sure that the future of quarrying at Coniston would not be helped by the estate being involved, except to receive annual rent ('dead money')

Brown Pike marks the end of the Coniston mountain chain. On the steep north-west facing slope of the mountain, just below the summit, are the remains of the Gold Scope slate workings (centre of photograph). Gold Scope worked a dark grey slate band. The only other location to work this band was the Common Wood Quarry in the Duddon Valley. The last proprietors of Gold Scope were the father and son team of Tom and Gordon Kendal. They worked the quarry alone for many years and Gordon continued for a short time after his father died.
Gold Scope was a very early site and was worked almost entirely by the 'cave-working' system where the slate band was 'followed' into the mountain from a point where it outcropped on the surface. The cave-working still exists. Photo – A Cameron

and royalties for the tonnage extracted from the operators. The leases would run for nine years.

The sale was held on Thursday 3rd May 1832 at 4pm at Coniston Old Hall. Earlier in the day Mr Anthony Gaskarth, who lived at the Old Hall, had conducted would be operators on a lightning tour of the quarries. The good Lady was obviously not satisfied with the results of the auction because, when the leases ran out in 1841 she decided to put them up for sale again rather than renew them to the lease holders as a formality. This time the sale was at the Black Bull in Coniston village. The landlord, Daniel Steele, was no doubt paid handsomely for his hospitality.

In 1844 plans were announced to build a railway, the first in the area, from Kirkby to Barrow, with a branch running to Rampside and Roa Island. The line was heavily promoted by both the Duke of Buccleuch and Lord Cavendish so that their iron ore and slate could be transported away easily.

Barrow was, at that time, a tiny hamlet. It had grown up around a small tidal harbour which had been used for many years for shipping local iron ore to South Wales. At Roa Island ships could berth at any state of the tide.

The grand opening of the line took place in 1846. Some years earlier, around the turn of the century, an inclined tramway had been built from Lord Cavendish's Kirkby quarry to the coast at Sandside. This tramway could now be used to carry slate directly from the quarry to the railway at Marshside where it would be transferred to the railway company's trucks. Lord William Cavendish had stolen quite a march on the Coniston slate industry which now faced another period of decline as a result. Coniston was still living in the horse-and-cart era and had little prospect of improving its lot for the foreseeable future. The reserves of slate at Kirkby were also vastly superior in size to those on the fells, and the slate deposits were much more predictable. But Coniston's saving grace was the colour and quality of its volcanic slate. As well as 'silver-grey' there were a great variety of shades of green and green/blue. Even in these early days, architects were already realising the attractiveness and durability of the product. It was much more desirable than the rather drab blue/grey sedimentary slate of Kirkby.

Coniston did not have to wait long for someone to take notice. In 1849 John Barraclough-Fell, the well known Furness contractor, announced that he was considering building a narrow gauge railway from Broughton to Coniston. The line was intended, primarily, to carry copper ore and slate. Although nothing of a material nature came of his plan it obviously started people thinking and eight years later, on 10th August 1857, the Coniston Railway Act received Royal Assent. The Coniston Railway was to be a standard gauge branch line. At least a quarter of the required initial capital was provided by Lady le Fleming and the lessees of the slate quarries and the Coniston Mine. On 18th June 1859, amidst great pomp and ceremony, the line was opened to passenger traffic. Two years earlier the

Furness Railway system had been connected to the West Coast Main Line at Carnforth. It was now possible to ship consignments of slate rapidly by rail from Coniston Station to most regions in the UK without using coastal shipping or canals. Modern times had arrived at last.

The opening of the Coniston branch didn't just assist local industry to expand. It also marked the start of the tourist boom. The Furness Railway Company were quick to realise the potential for this and soon special trains were bringing day trippers in their thousands to walk on the fells or sail in the Company's boats on the lake. But visitors had been travelling to Coniston for many years previously, although the journey had been somewhat tedious. In 1824 a small boy of five years old visited the village with his parents. He never forgot the place and over forty years later decided to make Coniston his home. He bought a cottage on the east side of the lake which he then proceeded to enlarge considerably. The cottage was called Brantwood and the new owner, John Ruskin, became a patron of many of the facilities in the village.

John Ruskin was one of several distinguished figures who made Coniston their home during the Victorian era. They had little contact with those who worked in the quarries and mines. It is strange, but probably understandable, that the two cultures knew little of each other's existence or way of life. On 7th March 1874 John Ruskin wrote in his diary, "*yesterday up Old Man, round under tarn, and down by soft grassy side to the south..........Remember the sensation at the slate quarry of standing unhappy.....and hearing the miner's slow pickaxe, or blasting stroke with dim echo, from underground; and thinking what his life was, compared with mine.*"

Although Ruskin had little direct contact with the quarrymen and miners, he took a keen interest in their leisure and cultural facilities. He became a patron and pillar of the Coniston Mechanics Institute and Literary Society which was designed to bring cultural and literary facilities to the workers. Over half of Coniston's total population was employed in the quarries and mines, and he obviously felt, like others, that they were in need of some cultural enlightenment. It must have been an uphill struggle at times. After a hard day's riving in the rain on the Old Man most quarrymen would want to do nothing more than sit in front of the fire at home or in the Black Bull. Nevertheless the 'Institute' became a centre for village life and benefited greatly from Ruskin's involvement. Later his secretary, W G Collingwood, was involved in setting up the museum behind the Institute which housed many mineral specimens that Ruskin had donated to the Society and, after his death, his personal belongings as well.

Within a matter of months the new railway started to have a major effect on the community. Quarry owners wasted little time in making use of the facility. The Cove and Banniside Slate Company (later to become the Coniston Slate Company) set up a slate stockyard at Torver Station. The Mandall Slate Company

Bait cabins or quarrymen's huts, such as this one on the fells above Tilberthwaite, were once a common site in the Coniston area. They provided a refuge from the mountain weather and somewhere for the men to eat their 'bait'. Very few of them have survived intact as this one does; most of them have lost their roofs long ago.
Recently the structure of this particular hut has been repaired and reinforced by local volunteers.

Photo – Peter Fleming

did the same at a purpose-built slate wharf at Coniston. Both these operations would now be able to compete nationally with rival concerns in other locations in England and Wales.

With the problems of transport finally overcome, the middle years of the 19th Century were good years with relative prosperity for those working in the quarries. In the 1860s quarry wages, meagre though they were, must have resulted in greater sums circulating monthly than, at the turn of the century, the area had seen in a year. These were boom times. The demand from the rapidly expanding towns and cities of industrial Britain frequently out-stripped supply. But none of the modern techniques of long term planning, forward forecasting and controlled expansion were known or even thought of in those days. Quarry proprietors just produced to their capacity. What they did not sell they stockpiled. Very regrettably the inevitable was to happen. The natural fluctuations of an industry with no strategic control were soon to take effect. During the mid 1870s prices began to waver. By the mid 1880s they had fallen by a third.

As the recession took hold many quarry proprietors 'battened down the hatches'. As always it was the quarry workers who were to suffer. At best the workings laid people off. At worst a few quarries closed completely. However, as often happens at these times, those operations which can ride out the bad times emerge at the end leaner and fitter and in a much healthier state to expand in the future. In the 1860s the industry was fragmented with at least eleven proprietors operating in the Coniston and Torver area alone. What was required was a degree of amalgamation and a strong, imaginative, up to date management style.

Several companies took a lead. The Mandall Company were already expanding. They were destined, for a number of decades at least, to become the leading greenslate quarry operator in Britain. As well as working the Old Man Quarries they also took over one of the Tranearth slab quarries at Torver and also the Blue Quarries above Coppermines Valley. Mandalls would continue to operate right up to the middle of the 20th Century. The Coniston Slate Company, with its headquarters at Outrake Farm, would not be so fortunate and have quite such a long life but, nevertheless, operated the Cove Quarry, Banniside slab quarry and also a slab quarry at Cat Bank above Coniston village. Both these operations will be described in detail later. At Tilberthwaite it would be a number of years before the various quarries were to be brought under one owner. In fact it was not until 1898 that the Buttermere Green Slate Company started getting interested in their southern competitors and took them under their wing.

As the turn of the century approached, slate prices started to recover. The industry was beginning to be placed on a modern footing even though, in 1896, the Cumbria area was only producing 4.4% of the total UK output; lower in fact than Scotland and Cornwall and about a tenth of that being produced by the Welsh industry.

This photograph was taken in about 1910 and shows a cart of slate leaving the Saddlestone Bank at the Old Man Quarries, heading for Coniston station. The route down from the quarries was, in some places, very steep. To help the descent a sledge was dragged behind the cart which acted as a brake on the steep slope with the added benefit that much more slate could be transported on each journey. The route was covered with a deep layer of slate rivings (chippings) which acted as a smooth surface on which the sledge could run. The lowest part of the route to Coniston station was on a public right of way and the damage caused to the road by sledges was an annoyance to Coniston residents. At the Coniston Parish Council meeting on November 9th 1901, councillors finally voted to outlaw the use of sledges completely. It didn't make any difference, the quarry operators continued to use them for many years.

Photo – Ruskin Museum archives

A few of the small operators would survive into the next century but, in the main it would be three companies that would progress, with the Mandall Company taking a lead.

The Mandall Slate Company

Anyone researching the history of the Coniston slate industry has great difficulty in obtaining anything but the scantiest details of the Mandall Company. Some reports suggest that Mandalls started working slate at Coniston in 1760. This was during the Rigg era and it is very unlikely that Mandalls would have been associated with William Rigg in working slate on the le Fleming lands. It is possible that they started on land to the south east of Torver Beck above Torver village. This area of land was owned by the Crown estates. In fact, in July 1870 a dispute arose between the lessees of the two workings at Tranearth. The Coniston Slate Company worked the Banniside Quarry on one side of Torver Beck on the le Flemings land while Thomas Mandall worked the Addyscale Quarry on the other side. This is one of the earliest reports we have of the activity of the Company but this date is over a hundred years after the Company is reported to have started.

Probably the most accurate guess that can be made is that the Mandall Company came into existence shortly after the Riggs ceased to be agents to the le Flemings, opening the doors for individuals to operate the quarries as they saw fit. During the le Fleming auctions of leases in 1841 they purchased the lease to the Old Man Quarries. Records suggest that, in doing so, they took over the whole of the quarrying operation on the north east flank of the mountain by taking on both Low Water Quarries and Scald Cop and adding these workings to Saddlestone and Moss Head Quarries which they had already been working for some time. These were all ancient workings, among some of the oldest in Britain. But despite their antiquity there was still plenty of slate to be won from the depths of Coniston Old Man by the Mandall Company.

The Saddlestone workings were on the silver-grey slate band. During the 1860s they consisted of an open quarry which ran into a large closehead. The workings were in the area known to present day quarrymen as Light Hole. Unfortunately we will never be able to examine these ancient workings. Within the past 50 years the original closehead has collapsed. The roof has caved in along the line of the 'slip' forming the southern wall of the chamber. It has taken with it the workings on the level below. The safety of the roof of the chamber had given Mandalls cause for concern on several occasions. In May 1899 they wrote to the estate informing them that rock was falling from the roof in no less than eight different places and operations at Saddlestone might have to be halted completely. There is no doubt that the original Saddlestone workings were very ancient and

A carter climbs the steep cart road to the main bank at Saddlestone on Coniston Old Man. He has nearly returned from delivering a load of slate to the Coniston station yard. Carters normally made three trips down from the quarries each day. This photograph was taken during the Summer of 1922.
Photo provided by Mrs P Tromans

certainly would have been in operation well before 1600 which would make them nearly as old as Scald Cop, above.

Scald Cop is about 600ft higher than Saddlestone. It is possible that Mandalls may have worked Scald Cop during the early years of their operation but certainly, by 1880, their monthly returns showed no slate extraction was taking place. Most of the workings at Scald Cop were underground and consisted of narrow, twisting tunnels within the slate band. These underground workings are fearsome places today. The rock is always on the move and they should never be entered.

Between Saddlestone and Scald Cop the workings at Moss Head were beginning to make a useful contribution to overall tonnage. As mentioned earlier, the two long levels at Moss Head had intersected the slate band after being driven for about 200ft through a sizable overburden of country rock. Moss Head became the first 'deep' slate mine in the area, possibly the country. It was to serve Mandalls well until the Old Man Quarries closed in 1959.

The Low Water Quarry has the distinction of being probably the highest slate mine in England. The quarry worked the silver-grey slate band where it outcropped on steep ground in the combe above Low Water Tarn. It is at an altitude of about 2300ft, only 300ft below the summit of the mountain. Although slate deposits at this point were small, the quality was excellent. But the difficult location meant that the quarry would never support more than two 'companies' of men. Mandalls constructed a cart road from their Saddlestone quarry, past Low Water Tarn and up the mountainside to the workings. This replaced an older and higher pack-horse track, remains of which can still be made out today.

In 1880 the Mandall Company signed yet another lease with Stanley Hughes le Fleming. There were two signatures for the Company, John Mandall and Thomas Mandall Clarke. The lease gave them the right to "*all of the quarries, mines and veins of stone and slate in, through and under so much of the surface lands of the Manor of Coniston.......as are unenclosed and the water from which flows into Copper Mines Beck.....*" The lease ran from May 1880 for a further twenty years. In particular they had to "*keep employed twenty labouring men at least in digging, searching for and getting the slate unless prevented therefrom by storms or bad weather.*" They also had to "*work quarries at not less than four different places according to the best techniques.*" There was a lot of argument over the use of sledges on the roads down to Coniston and they had to agree they did not damage the road down from the copper mines to the Copper House at the head of the railway. Clearly the le Flemings were concerned that nothing should get in the way of the operation of the copper mines.

Once the lease had been signed Mandalls embarked on another major development. The technique they had developed at Moss Head of driving deep levels through the non-slate rock to intersect the slate band deep underground had

27

This riving shed at the Sandbeds workings above Tilberthwaite was large enough to hold two rivers and dressers, showing that the site was felt to hold great prospects. Unfortunately history shows that this was not to be the case and Sandbeds closed between the wars. Since this photograph was taken the shed has collapsed.
Photo provided by Peter Fleming

been very successful. They therefore decided to do the same much lower down the mountain, below the existing Saddlestone workings. Work progressed intermittently on two new levels and it was not until about 1888 that, after about 200ft, both struck good slate 'metal'. Today these levels are known as Smithy Bank and Saddlestone Main Bank. Their development had been successful and for the next fifty years both would be worked extensively.

Three years later Mandalls embarked on another similar project to drive a further level to exploit the ground between the Main Bank and the small closehead of Brandy Crag several hundred feet below. This level became known as Low Bank and was also destined to be a success.

For a few years from 1880 Mandalls also worked a small trial which was locally known as Moor Quarry. These workings are situated at Kitty Crag on the moorland between Coppermines Valley and Tilberthwaite. During 1881 Moor Quarries were making a considerable contribution to tonnage. Whereas Saddlestone was producing an average of 80 tons/month of 'best' slates, Moor was producing 15 tons. Mandalls could not have employed more than one company of men at Moor and by the turn of the century work was only occasional.

Below Moor Quarry on the sides of the Coppermines Valley Mandalls were also developing Blue Quarry. In June 1896 Thomas Mandall reported to the estate: *"Our floor at Blue Quarry is turning out badly. I fear we are not going to find anything. There is plenty of slate rock but not a bit of good bate in it. We have laid out up to present over £400."* Clearly Blue Quarry was considered important to them. Unlike all their workings over on Coniston Old Man, the quarry worked the light green slate band. *"Architects want a greener slate. This cuts us dreadfully, Saddlestone slate being simply short of the green tinge."*

Despite their continuing development Mandalls were feeling the effects of the 1880s slump in trade. At the end of 1883 they reported that *"upon the whole the trade is in a wretched state. We only just broke even in 1882."* In 1884 things were not getting any better. *"Trade is yet very dull. Sorry we have such poor returns. Hope times may soon improve although I don't think we shall have much doing until we have a change of Government. All confidence seems to have been destroyed throughout the country."* The following year things did in fact start to improve. In one of his reports Thomas Mandall remarked that *"a better month this, hope it may continue. This is a Tory month, the last was a Liberal one. Low Water is still making a good contribution for us........."*

As the turn of the century approached the lease for their quarries was again renewed with the estate. The Lords of the Manor were clearly very satisfied that, at last, someone was working the quarries in an innovative and businesslike way. During the past half century the Company had managed to ride out the depression in the trade, had worked the quarries professionally and had shown considerable innovation especially in the successful development of deep underground closeheads within Coniston Old Man. They now started to give serious thoughts to tackling a number of long-term problems that had concerned them for several years, including the transport of products down the mountainside, the provision of electricity and compressed air at the Old Man workings and the problem of trying to make the Blue Quarry pay.

The Buttermere Green Slate Company
It wasn't just the Coniston area that suffered from the slate depression of the 1880s. The slump had affected the whole country. In Wales, at Penrhyn, Dinorwic and Blaenau Ffestiniog, the recession devastated whole communities which were far more dependent on slate quarrying than at Coniston. In the Lake District the area which appears to have suffered most was Honister.

Slate has been quarried and mined from Honister Crag since well before 1700, but when the depression took hold, the workings at Honister came to a complete halt and remained so for about ten years. Close by, on the other side of Honister Hause, the Yew Crag workings also virtually shut down.

But in 1878 three extremely resourceful and progressive partners, Messrs Barrett, Salmon and Sawrey, started to take an interest in this area. The Egremont Estates granted them the lease to work part of Yew Crag in May 1879. In 1881 they also took over the lease for Honister Crag. The new operation was to become the Buttermere Green Slate Company. For the next twenty years they were to expand the Honister site, construct tramways up the crag face and develop the underground mining areas. By 1895 they had been joined by Mr Bennett Johns, another extremely energetic and resourceful figure. The Company was obviously on a very sound footing and, in 1898, the partners started to look round the district for other possible acquisitions.

They didn't have to look for long. The slate workings at Tilberthwaite were still being run by a number of proprietors, one of whom was Bennett Johns himself who had worked the Broad Moss Quarry. Clearly this whole area had vast reserves of rock but there was a lack of co-ordination between the operators. They were still operating independently as they had for several centuries. Tilberthwaite had not yet benefited from the 'Mandall' style.

For many years Hodge Close Quarry itself had been worked as a number of separate undertakings, all leased from the Dukes of Buccleuch. In 1866 John Nevison of Langdale leased 'Great Parrock Quarry' and in the same year Charles Parker of Hall Garth leased 'Great Low Quarry'. Four years later John Burns of Stang End took up the lease of 'Lightend Quarry', John Birkett leased 'Lords Quarry' and Isaac Rigg, 'Fell Quarry'. All these workings were at Hodge Close but few of the names are known today and we can only guess as to their location. The Dukes of Buccleuch were very keen to maintain the quarries in working order and even paid the lease-holders up to 5d per ton for clearing away their own rubbish.

Fred 'Skinner' Walker dresses slate in his riving shed at Hodge Close Quarry in 1936. Fred was a skilled worker and could dress many dozens of slates an hour. Consequently dressers such as Fred would be shared amongst several 'companies' of men, receiving payment from each for their work. On the left of this picture rough slates are stacked ready for dressing by Fred while finished slates are neatly stacked on the right.
Photo – Mrs M E Rawes

At this time all the Duke's affairs were carried out by his agent Edward Wadham who was based at Dalton in Furness.

It isn't proposed to list all the proprietors that have worked the ground in Tilberthwaite during the 19th Century. However an important sale took place on Thursday 18th August 1893 when the main Hodge Close workings changed hands. The previous proprietor, a Mr Robinson, had decided to retire and the lease was sold to a Mr Shenton of Derby. Mr Charles Parker had, by this time, become the manager at Hodge Close. He had moved to nearby Stang End. He was re-appointed by the new lease holders and his experience would no doubt be invaluable. As a 'thank you' from the former owner, the men at the quarry were treated to supper at the Black Bull on the following Saturday evening.

During the 1870s Hodge Close had started to become an extensive undertaking. A number of long levels had been driven from lower ground in the woodland to try and intersect the light green band. One level had been successful and after some considerable distance had struck what was to be a massive deposit. This was soon exploited and worked as an underground closehead beneath the existing open working. Eventually the roof of the closehead was removed and the whole operation was worked as an open pit. In 1885 a fall of rock estimated at being over 1000 tons occurred at Hodge Close. No one was hurt but two men had a narrow escape and the fall took away the boundary fence. Another major fall happened five years later and a considerable amount of equipment including a steam crane ended up at the bottom of the pit.

Nearby, the Parrock Quarry was being worked by separate proprietors. This was also, originally, an underground closehead. The entrance to the chamber was by a long tunnel which ran for nearly 300 yards into the closehead from beneath Parrock Bank to the north west. As with Hodge Close, the roof was subsequently removed and the quarry worked as an open pit. It wasn't long before the 300 yard level was abandoned. An inclined tramway was installed and slate was lifted from the floor of the pit by the tramway, remains of which can still be seen on the north side. Eventually the Parrock Quarry became joined to Hodge Close when part of the intervening face was removed to form an arch.

By 1897 Hodge Close had once again changed hands. By now the workings had become The Tilberthwaite Green Slate Company and the new proprietors were James Stephenson & Co. The manager was Mr J J Thomas from Little Langdale. The same company also, at that time, operated Moss Rigg.

In 1898 the Buttermere Green Slate Company had stepped in and taken over Parrock. They also absorbed a number of the smaller Tilberthwaite workings including Sty Rigg and Broad Moss. They were soon to take over Moss Rigg as well.

At last quarrying at Tilberthwaite was being put on an organised basis. There would be no more frequent changing of proprietors. Over the next twenty

Beneath the tips at Hodge Close a group of rivers and dressers work in their riving shed. The river on the right is using a mallet and chisel to split the slate, a method that was introduced from the Welsh slate industry at the turn of the century. The two men on the left are using the traditional Lakeland riving hammer which required a great deal more skill but gave a much better result. The seated gentleman with straw boater is the dresser. He is trimming the slates to size with his 'whittle' and 'brake'. The large wooden mallets in the foreground were known as 'mells'. They were made of yew and were used for 'docking' (splitting) clogs of slate. The men were probably part of the same 'Company' of six men. The two not in the photograph would be the rockhands who worked the face.

Photo – Ruskin Museum archives

years the Buttermere Company would take over and work these quarries as a satellite of their Honister operation and provide steady employment for nearly half a century.

For the quarrymen who worked at Tilberthwaite the future prospects seemed bright. The working conditions were relatively good when compared to those at the high, rain-lashed quarries on Coniston Old Man. Many of them lived at Holme Ground and Little Langdale, communities which were only a few minutes walk away from work. Not for them the tramp up the mountain by the light of storm lanterns on dark frosty mornings. But working at the Tilberthwaite quarries had one major drawback. The injury rate was extremely high and the last decade of the 19th Century saw, on average, one major accident a month occurring. Why this should be is not certain. One possible explanation is that the process of 'open-topping', i.e. removing the roof of closeheads, was a particularly hazardous one. Because of the gently sloping ground it was much more feasible to operate as an open-top quarry in the Tilberthwaite valley than it was on steep mountain sides. But not all the injuries were caused by rock falls. Several were the result of blasting accidents. Coniston's doctor, Dr Kendall, was kept extremely busy and his horse must have known its way up to Tilberthwaite blindfolded. If we take one year at random, 1898, and analyse the incidents, the hazardous nature of the work will become apparent.

The year of 1898 had only just started when the first accident occurred. On Saturday January 8th William Coward was working at Moss Rigg preparing a shot hole. He had inserted the powder and lit the fuse. As he walked away the charge exploded prematurely. The blast caught him in the back of his thigh and threw him to the ground. He had a very severe flesh wound and bled profusely. His mates lifted him onto a slate cart and drove him home to Coniston where Dr Kendall treated him. Less than a month later two quarrymen were hurt by a large fall of rock at Parrock. They received severe injuries but fortunately both of them recovered.

On three consecutive days in March of that year accidents also occurred. The most serious was on March 13th when Daniel Hogan was badly injured at Hodge Close and subsequently died. He had been opening a cask of black powder and was using a hammer and chisel to try and remove one of the metal bands. A spark from the chisel landed on the powder and there was a huge explosion. The inquest was held at the Black Bull on the following Tuesday. The day after this incident, an apprentice by name of Shaw was standing on a ledge at the Penny Rigg Quarry when it gave way and he fell to the quarry floor. He was a very lucky lad as he only received a cut to the head. Fortunately the same was also true for John Dixon of Lake View, Coniston, the following day. He was at the top of a ladder at Penny Rigg boring a shot hole when a quantity of rock fell from higher up the face smashing the ladder to pieces and throwing him to the quarry floor.

Although he received severe cuts and bruising he was able to walk home after resting for an hour or two.

More incidents occurred in April. On the 12th two men were badly hurt at Moss Rigg when a fall of rock struck them. One of them, John Shaw of Tarn Hows, was working on a ladder. His mate, a Cornishman called Carnes, was working at the foot. Both were caught by the fall. Dr Kendall was summoned and attended to their injuries where they lay after the debris had been removed. The men were taken home by cart and, later that day, Carnes was taken on to Barrow hospital for treatment.

Four days later one of the most serious accidents in the area for many years occurred at Parrock Quarry. John Bond was a highly respected quarryman who originated from Cornwall. He had moved to Cumberland and had worked for a number of years at Honister before coming to Coniston. On April 16th 1898 he was working on the face at Parrock when an enormous quantity of rock fell, completely covering him. His mate had a very narrow escape. He was just walking away at the time to get a powder straw. The rock had fallen from the old chamber roof which was in the process of being removed and as no one actually saw it happen it was difficult to say exactly where the body lay. During the night another huge fall occurred. Work continued day and night to locate and remove the body but it was not until May 28th, over five weeks later, that it was found. The body was removed the following morning before day-break to a barn at Cat Bank. Work to locate it had been badly hampered by sightseers who lined the quarry rim to view the scene and slate production at the quarry all but halted during this period.

And so the year went on. Accidents involving blasting and rock falls continued to occur frequently. In total nineteen people were injured in the Tilberthwaite area alone that year compared to two at Mandall's quarries on the Old Man. The risks didn't just involve quarrymen, but their families as well. During a Saturday evening in June six small boys from Holme Ground were playing in the woods near to the quarry. They had managed to obtain some black powder and had placed it in an old drilling hole. They inserted a straw fuse and lit it. Nothing happened. One of the boys became impatient and went back to the hole to blow the fuse gently as he assumed it had gone out. The resulting explosion badly scorched his face, and that of his younger brother who was standing behind him.

Although the Buttermere Company was beginning to absorb many of the Tilberthwaite workings, the Hodge Close quarry remained under the control of Messrs James Stephenson well into the 20th Century. In fact it was only after the First World War that Buttermere was able to get their hands on this valuable asset, and then only after a series of disasters at the quarry had crippled the Stephensons financially. At the turn of the century however, Hodge Close was very prosperous.

35

Work had been completed to take off the closehead roof and the depth of the quarry was increasing month by month.

In 1899 the Company installed and commissioned a water balance lift which was designed to raise slate clog from the quarry floor as far as a landing at the end of the former access level. From here it was taken along the level and out to 'day' to be riven and dressed in riving sheds on the lower banks. The installation was very effective except that, as the quarry depth grew, it became more and more difficult to transport clog to the base of the lift. Eventually the lift was abandoned and dismantled. It was replaced by a 'blondin' lift, the design and operation of which will be described in the next chapter.

Mr J Thomas, the manager at Hodge Close was a well respected man. The men at the quarry had a great regard for him as did the community in general. He was, for several years, county councillor for the Oldhallows district of Kendal. Sadly he was not a well man. He appeared to suffer from recurring bouts of dizziness. On one occasion, while at the quarry, he was standing on the edge watching the work going on below when he overbalanced and fell. Fortunately he landed on a ledge about 25ft down from where the men were able to retrieve him. He was taken, quite badly injured, to a nearby house to await the arrival of Dr Kendall.

Coniston Slate Company

Mr C H B Cane was land agent at the Rydal Estate office in Ambleside between 1865 and 1903. He was a neat, particular man who detested chaos. He administered the estate at a difficult period and found that much of his time was taken up with sorting out problems with the copper and slate industries. The Coniston Copper Mine was in serious decline and the slate quarries, whose fortunes fluctuated year after year, needed his constant attention.

Of the major slate companies that paid royalties to the Estate, both Mandalls and the Buttermere Company always presented good accounts, neatly laid out, and were always able to justify the royalties they paid by referring to tonnage figures and their records of sales. Sadly the same was not true for the Coniston Slate Company.

The Company's origins go back to 1843 when three men, Joseph Jackson of Lowick, Edward Coward of Kirkby and James Frearson of Grizebeck applied successfully to the estate to take up the lease on Cove Quarries high on Coniston Old Man. This green slate quarry had already become very extensive but had, recently, run into problems of poor rock. The group also worked the sedimentary slates of Banniside Quarry (Tranearth) above Torver. The main product from this quarry was flags and, for many years, the Company was referred to as the "Cove and Flag Quarry" but eventually became the Coniston Slate Company. Later, the Company acquired the Cat Bank Slab Quarry above Coniston village.

A group of quarrymen and boys take a few minutes out to be photographed in one of the riving sheds at Moss Rigg. The group are displaying the tools of their trade including the traditional Lakeland riving hammer, the 'imported' mallet and chisel and the 'big mell' used for docking clogs of slate.
Photo provided by Doug Birkett

Edward Coward acted as a working general manager during the early years. He abhorred paperwork and had no intention of keeping important documents safe in neat files. Like quarrymen over the years he would go to great lengths to comment on the poor market conditions, the high wages he had to pay, the problems he had locating good slate at the quarry, the level of royalties, the cost of transport and the condition of the road down from Tranearth. There is no doubt that Mr Cane at the estate office found him intolerable. Letters would never be answered, rent and royalties would not be paid on time and it was usually impossible to justify the royalty sum with dispatched tonnage.

However Edward Coward was shrewd and would never miss an opportunity to 'off-load' paperwork. When the railway to Coniston opened the local industry found a ready means of carrying goods very efficiently. The Cove and Flag Quarry was quick to make use of this new facility. Torver station yard made a very useful stock yard for slate, although there is every possibility that the Furness Railway Company had great difficulty in obtaining payment from them as well. Mr Coward was aware that David Walker, the new station master at Torver, had once been a river at Cove Quarries and therefore knew the different qualities and sizes of slate. Soon the station master found he had an additional duty to perform, that of book keeper for his former boss. Mr Coward presented him with a large book in which he asked him to record the number of tons, the quality and the destination of all slates passing through Torver. When the next royalty payment was questioned by the Estate, Mr Coward suggested that Mr Cane should take a trip to Torver station and check the records for himself.

During the 1860s the Coniston Slate Company found ready sale for their slates and flags from the slab quarry. At that time some areas of Low and Middle Cove Quarries were being developed but results were not promising, a fact which Edward Coward was quick to point out to the Estate. Two levels had been driven into the south west flank of Coniston Old Man at Middle Cove but had met unsuitable rock. *"We are much troubled with white flints in the slate"* he had written to Mr Cane. As if to reinforce their problems he added *"I never knew slate quarrymen so scarce and so high wages given. We shall have to build some houses at Torver to keep the men."*

The flag quarry at Banniside however appeared to hold much better prospects. In 1867 new lifting machinery was installed and in 1870 the Estate was notified that the Company were planning to construct a water race from Torver Beck to turn a wheel which would drive a saw to cut flags. Two years later the Company drove a new low level into the quarry which was, at that time, worked as a closehead. Having completed the level the quarry was then opened out to the surface.

Although Banniside was working well, the situation up at Cove was not getting any better. In 1872 no men at all had been hired to work there and, for a period of six months, the quarry closed down completely.

By 1874, however, some work had restarted. But it was not continuous, although where a good pocket of slate was found it would be worked enthusiastically. The silver-grey slate band on Coniston Old Man had always produced high quality slate for riving and it was probably this reason that prompted the Company to have another go at improving the fortunes at Cove.

During the late 1870s it was decided to prospect on the steep mountainside at a higher altitude than the existing workings. Here the silver-grey band outcropped but this was only evident to the experienced eye. Glacial action and the effects of the weather had shattered the surface rock. There was good potential but great practical difficulties. In this high and exposed place, it would be necessary to build a cart road up from the previous highest access point on towards the summit of the mountain on what is probably its steepest side. A flat working floor would have to be constructed and riving sheds built. Despite the difficult location the work was completed. By 1881 rock with an excellent bate was once more being obtained and fine slates were being riven. The tonnage of made slates leaving Torver station rose from a meagre 24 tons in 1872 to 271 tons in 1881. The prospect looked good, but in quarrying, as in mining, the future can never be certain. By 1891 the dispatches from Cove had again fallen to 54 tons and by 1896 this remote and inaccessible part of the Coniston Fells once more fell silent. Despite a further attempt the following year, no more extraction has taken place to the present day at the Upper Cove quarry.

The 1890s heralded a period of change for the Coniston Slate Company. Mr John Haimer joined the consortium and was soon followed by Mr John Bowness, who had been involved in the operation of the small Outrake Quarry at Coniston. Mr Edward Coward retired due to ill health. Clearly the need to understand business systems and finances did not suit him. The Company address was now Outrake, Coniston. The style of the new management contrasted well with the bumbling systems of the old timers and output of the Banniside flag quarry reflected this.

It didn't take the Fleming Estate long to realise this either and, in 1891, they informed the Company that they wished to increase the annual rent and the royalty revenue. The Company had difficulty in arguing against this. Poor book-keeping in the past meant that there were no accurate records of tons dispatched. Even the records of the Torver station master could not be regarded as a fully accurate picture. In the end it was proposed by the Estate that a 5% increase in royalties would be applied. Mr Haimer ultimately agreed, there was little else he could do. He was quick to point out however that there was very keen competition within their market from competitors including Caithness and Yorkshire flags.

Fred Brownlee and two apprentices rive slates on the quarry bank at Hodge Close in about 1932. There were several sheds on the bank, each used by a different Company of men. After the Second World War they were all demolished and replaced by a corrugated iron building known locally as The Hangar.

Photo – Mrs M E Rawes

The Banniside quarry was by now in full production. Included in the product list were flags, lintels, steps, sills, gate posts and walling stone. In 1891 a total of 470 tons of prepared product was carried by cart down the fellside from Tranearth to Torver station. Two years later the total was well over 600 tons. Customers for the Company products were not just local merchants. Slate was being shipped throughout the north of England and to many locations in Scotland.

Unfortunately the road down to Torver from the quarry continued to be a problem. With the increased output the number of journeys by horse and cart made each day also increased. The route crossed the beck close to Tranearth Farm by a ford. It then ran along the fellside for about half a mile and then descended towards the valley, reaching it at the small group of dwellings known as Scar Head. The descent was steep. The surface of the road was extremely poor. Despite attempts by the Company to improve the road, it remained a problem until the workings closed down.

Whereas Banniside was becoming a very successful operation, the same could not be said for the Company's other flag quarry at Cat Bank above Coniston village. This working was in fact producing over 400 tons a year but the very congested site and major disagreements with the Estate created problems for the Coniston Slate Company for several years.

Cat Bank Quarry was situated just above the top terrace of houses in the village. In 1896 the Company had to purchase six cottages close to the mouth of the quarry. This course of action was found to be necessary as the owners were threatening to serve an injunction on the Company to make them cease operating. They also had to purchase more land for tipping and build large retaining walls. There were never more than three men working at the quarry and none of the partners in the Coniston Slate Company received any profit at all from the Cat Bank operation.

All the above points were put very forcibly to the Estate in 1896 when it was announced that they intended to double the annual rent asked for the quarry. Mr Haimer wasted no time in confronting them and even suggested that they were looking at production figures from the wrong quarry. The Estate were not prepared to justify the increase. There were others in Coniston who would jump at the chance to take over the quarry and Mr Haimer reluctantly gave in and accepted the new rent. Perhaps this was a mistake. Markets were changing. Within a very few decades the production of flags for floors was to decline. Other items such as steps and sills could be manufactured easily as a by-product at the big green slate quarries at Tilberthwaite and on the Old Man.

Because of the dangerous nature of the work, accidents were a fact of life in the slate quarries. The Coniston Slate Company was involved in a particularly serious incident at Banniside in 1901. On August 1st a young rock hand, Ben Cooper from Thurston Bank, was working part-way down a face when the rope to

41

which he was attached slipped from its mooring iron at the top of the face. Cooper fell to the quarry floor and was killed. The inquest was held at the Sun Hotel, Coniston four days later. The coroner, Mr Poole, heard evidence from the foreman, John Barrow, his workmates and also from Mr Haimer. The jury returned a verdict of accidental death but recommended that bars used for mooring should be better designed.

In 1898 the Company abandoned their lease to Cove. However there will always be those who are prepared to take a risk and the Estate received a number of inquiries later that year, both from local people and from as far away as Darlington and Scotland. Although the 1912 edition of the Ordnance Survey shows Cove as being abandoned, it continued to be worked from time to time during the first two decades of the 20th Century. The Broughton Moor Slate Company operated it in the early 1920s employing four men who probably only worked the closeheads of the Low Quarry. But by 1935 the workings had closed down completely.

Because of the unique location of Cove the abandoned buildings soon found a new use for outdoor pursuits. Less than a mile away is the well known climbing area of Dow Crag. The walk up to Dow from Torver station usually took a good hour and a half and a group of climbers from Barrow realised that the now-disused powder magazine at the quarries could make an ideal base which was only a few minutes away from the foot of their favourite crag. The climbers took the building over and it became known as Cove Hut. It was equipped with sleeping accommodation and was used for over thirty years, providing a dry refuge in which to spend the night. Sadly, now, the building has been abandoned. Another building on the main quarry bank was taken over by Mr Jack Diamond, a Coniston schoolmaster and keen mountaineer. This building is still in use as a mountain 'bothy'.

In the 1920s the lease for Banniside and the adjoining Addyscale Quarries was taken up by Mandall Ltd. Very little further work has been done at either site since.

The end of the century
In the last four years of the 19th Century slate prices recovered strongly. The depression in the industry was over for the time being at least. This was extremely fortunate for the community of Coniston as the Coniston Copper Mine was virtually at the end of its life. By 1890 returns were low and it was difficult to persuade the financial backers to invest without a reasonable certainty of some return, and all the surveys suggested that the prospects were not good. Commercially the Coniston Mine was exhausted. For a number of years men had been drifting away. Some found employment in the slate quarries. The Coniston railway provided a degree of mobility and those living in Coniston were able to

The old gunpowder magazine at Low Cove was taken over by a local group of mountaineers once Cove Quarries closed. This photograph shows Jim Cameron, a local mountain guide, and a client packing their rucksacks at the front door of the building in preparation for a days climbing on Dow Crags. The building was substantially built and timber lined to protect kegs of black powder from the damp during storage.   *Photo – A Cameron, source unknown*

travel down to work at the rich iron ore mines of Low Furness or Hodbarrow at Millom. Others moved away completely, finding some employment in the lead mines at Patterdale and in the Northern Pennines and at least six Coniston miners decided to emigrate to the 'new world'.

During these difficult times the copper mine was being operated by the Coniston Mining Syndicate under the direction of Thomas Warsop. In 1892 he took the unenviable decision to stop the pumps which, effectively, meant that the mine would start to fill with water. It couldn't have been an easy decision for Thomas Warsop to make. Once the mine filled above a certain level the process would be irretrievable. Never again would copper be wrought from the depths of the Coniston Mine. The lowest workings were known as the 205 Fathom Level, and were well below sea level.

The pumps were actually stopped during April of that year but it was not until 1897 that the water level finally reached Deep Level, the lowest drainage point, and started to pour out of the adit mouth and into the beck. During the intervening years some copper was obtained as the pillars of ore left in by the miners for safety in previous decades were removed. Most surprisingly, during this five year period, slate was also mined from outcrops amongst the veins of copper. At two points the miner's levels had cut through bands of silver-grey slate. One was in Taylor's Level, the entrance of which is mid way between the Coppermines Valley and Red Dell. The second is in an area which has only recently been revisited at the eastern extremity of Deep Level. In 1894 approximately 50 tons were produced and more than double that was dressed in 1895. No slate at all was obtained in 1897 and it is assumed that, by this time, the old mine workings had become too unsafe to work for slate.

The mystery and anticipation of the next century must have tantalised the people of Coniston. Would the 1900s bring new fortunes? Or would it bring even more hardship, poverty and emigration. In the event it is unlikely that anyone could have foreseen the next hundred years; the complete closure of the Coniston Copper Mine, of Mandall's Quarries and the Coniston railway, the dramatic decline in requirement for slate for roofing and the explosive rise in tourism. But all would not be gloom. During the next 60 years two Coniston companies would emerge to become world leaders in the supply of architectural slate for cladding and would, by the middle of the century, be supplying their products for some of the most prestigious building projects right across the globe.

THE TWENTIETH CENTURY

Coniston celebrated the start of the new century very quietly with little fuss and ceremony. The church bells were rung to welcome in the New Year and many working people made New Year's Day a holiday. The Coniston Brass Band played and a choral recital was performed at the Wesleyan chapel. The community was confident; employment worries were far from its mind.

The village was becoming established as a literary and artistic centre and it was also seeing tourism starting to develop in earnest. The number of hotels and boarding houses taking in visitors was increasing, many were travelling to the village to enjoy the facilities that the area provided. Fishing in the rivers and on the lake was becoming popular as was hill walking. Rock climbers were becoming frequent visitors, enjoying the facilities provided by Dow Crag and other local crags. One of Britain's foremost rock climbing clubs, The Fell and Rock Climbing Club, had its inaugural meeting at the Sun Hotel, Coniston, on November 11th 1906. Coniston was experiencing its first taste of a tourist and leisure boom that would continue expanding steadily up to the present day.

The century had hardly started before two deaths occurred in Coniston in the same week. Both had a profound effect on the village, but in different ways. *The Westmorland Gazette* of January 22nd 1900 reported the death of John Ruskin, Coniston's social patron. He had died at his home, Brantwood, the previous Saturday afternoon. The following day Mr Moses Barrow, under manager at Hodge Close, also died. Whereas Ruskin's fame was international, few outside the South Lakeland valleys had heard of Moses Barrow. But the death of Mr Barrow was felt greatly. He was a quiet but natural leader of the workforce at the quarry. To the younger employees he was looked upon as a strong father figure, always respected and his judgment never questioned. He was buried at Langdale and virtually the whole of the Hodge Close workforce, and many from other quarries as well, walked over to Langdale to attend the funeral. His grave was marked by a simple headstone of slate from the quarry. John Ruskin was buried at Coniston after lying in state for several days. Special trains were laid on to bring all who wished to attend and also carry the vast quantities of flowers and wreaths to the village. Ruskin's grave is marked by an intricately carved gravestone, the shaft and head originating from Moss Rigg and the base from Elterwater Quarry.

At the start of the new century Coniston village was relatively prosperous, despite the decline of the copper mines. Slate prices remained strong for a number of years. By 1903 they had regained their 1876 levels. This was due in part to the infamous Penrhyn Stoppages, a series of strikes and acts of retaliation by the management that took place between 1900 and 1903. The major shortfall in supply

General scene on the main bank of Hodge Close in the 1940s.
Photo – Ruskin Museum archives

from this huge Welsh quarry benefited the Coniston slate industry greatly. But this would not last for ever. More natural fluctuations in the industry coupled with Penrhyn coming back on stream in 1904 was destined to produce another slump and by 1906 prices were down again to those of the lean years of the 1880s.

Markets were changing as well. Demand for products from Coniston's slab quarries, which had given so much steady employment during the previous century, was now declining. More Coniston men decided to emigrate and seek a better life in the new world. In one week alone in June 1907 nine men and their families departed. One of these was Mr George Bains who had worked for 14 years at Mandalls and 18 years at Hodge Close. He and his brother Tom sailed on June 6th for British Columbia.

The 1906 slump also marked the end for some of the smaller greenslate quarries in less accessible locations. A number of the larger workings such as Walna Scar which had been in operation for many hundreds of years also closed down. Several other quarries would keep operating for a few more years, but at marginal costs and with a very small workforce. These included Gold Scope high on the north east flank of Brown Pike, the Tranearth, Cat Bank and Guards slab quarries, Low Water, Penny Rigg and Goats Crag in Tilberthwaite and Mandall's Moor Quarry above the Coppermines Valley.

Gold Scope was one of the oldest 'green' slate quarries in Britain and had worked its own dark slate band more or less continuously by surface and underground techniques for centuries. Gold Scope slate was unique. The only other location to have worked this particular band of slate was at Common Wood in Dunnerdale. It was reputed to be very difficult to cleave and could only be worked really well using the traditional riving hammer.

The last proprietor of Gold Scope was Gordon Kendal who lived at High Ground midway between Torver and Coniston. Gordon's father, Tom, worked the quarry during the early years of the century. Gordon himself had embarked on a career with the Ordnance Survey and was based for many years at Southampton. Before this, however, he had helped his father at the quarry. Tom Kendal refused to buy anything that he could make himself. Consequently they made their own tools and even their own slater's ladders, obtaining supplies of 'ladder-larch' from the woods of Colwith. Occasionally, when necessary, they would employ two or three local quarrymen but in the main they worked the quarry alone. When Tom became too old to continue, Gordon carried on himself for a number of years until Gold Scope was eventually closed and he embarked on his career as a surveyor. When Gordon retired he returned to the family home at Coniston.

Gold Scope now stands silent, the haunt of foxes and ravens. When one visits this high and remote place it is easy to imagine that the spirits of the father and son team are still there, working the face, riving and dressing the slate and loading the cart for the long trek back down to Torver.

Two other workings to struggle on for a few years were Penny Rigg and Goats Crag. They were on the slopes of Yewdale Crags in the Tilberthwaite Valley. Despite being very close to each other they appeared to have worked different slate bands. Penny Rigg worked the silver-grey band and Goats Crag the light green band. Both had been in operation during the late 1700s. Penny Rigg had developed into a sizable working. A series of small underground chambers had broken into each other and the roof subsequently removed to form an elongated, open pit.

There are conflicting reports of the history of Penny Rigg. Eric Holland, in his field guide to Coniston Copper Mines describes the Penny Rigg quarry as being abandoned by 1875. He believes that, later, the open pit was used as a reservoir for the adjacent Penny Rigg Copper Mill. A level referred to as Quarry Adit was driven from the base of the pit through the shoulder of the fell to emerge close to the copper mill where it drove a 32ft diameter water wheel. Remains of the wheel pit can be seen today. However in 1881 Mr Bennett Johns was in negotiation with the Fleming Estates over Penny Rigg. He was keen to take on the lease to quarry slate but *"we have not had much success although Penny Rigg may eventually pay someone pretty well."* In 1892 Thomas Warsop, inventor and engineer, and for several years involved in the Coniston Mine, took over and re-opened Penny Rigg. In 1912 the quarry was still working, possibly via a close head at the western end. It was eventually abandoned in the 1930s when the proprietors were listed as the Shaw family.

Mr Bennett Johns was a shrewd and clever mining engineer. He originated from Ulverston and, for nearly ten years, was agent at the Coniston Mine. He moved to Keswick in 1884 and was then involved for a further time with the Buttermere Green Slate Company. He was instrumental in acquiring many of the Tilberthwaite quarries for the Buttermere Company. He also, during 1900, had his eye on Blue Quarry with which Mandalls were still experiencing problems and were considering abandoning.

In May 1900 Bennett Johns wrote to the le Fleming Estates inquiring about the lease for Blue Quarry. He stressed that his inquiries were 'for a friend only'. At first the estate misunderstood him and assumed that he was referring to Moor Quarries. Eventually the confusion was sorted out and a dialogue started. Bennett Johns informed the estate that he proposed to assess the possibility of driving a level from the foot of the lowest spoil tip of Low Blue Quarry to develop the band at a lower depth.

Four months later the estate received another inquiry about Blue Quarry, this time from Mr Thomas Knipe of Thurston Bank asking whether it was to be let. A month after this Bennett Johns reported on his investigations. The cost of driving the level was, he estimated, between £500 and £600. *"I cannot advise my friends to run the risk. The previous tenants should have kept the road open on the level of the smithy floor so that intending applicants could see the condition of the*

Owner and postal address	Name of mine	Situation	Agent	Persons u/g	a/g
Buttermere Green Slate Co	Dubbs	Honister	B. Johns	*	*
	Honister	"	"	25	31
	Quay Foot	Borrowdale	"	2	2
	Yew Craggs	Honister	"	*	*
	High Fellside	nr. Coniston	"	6	6
	* denotes that persons employed in these locations are included in totals for Honister				
Wm Casson Ltd., Ulpha	Common Wood	Ulpha	Wm Casson	1	1
Cumberland Green Slate Co	Rigg Head	Borrowdale	E Rushforth	2	2
Broughton Moor Slate Co	Cove	Coniston	H Mellon	-	4
Ghyll Slate Co.	Horse Crag	Tilberthwaite	J W Shaw	2	1
Mandall's Slate Co Ltd	Saddlestone & Spion Cop	Coniston	J Poole	16	34
Tilberthwaite Green Slate Co Ltd	Hodge Close	Coniston	J J Thomas	7	13
	Jumb Quarry	Kentmere	"	8	2
	Steelrigg	"	"	(not worked in 1923)	

Reproduction of part of the 1923 Annual Statistics

rock." He added that "*it would be difficult to drive the level under the old floor and leave sufficient tip room above the road leading to Irish Cottages.*"

Shortly after Bennett Johns' report, Mandalls decided not to abandon Blue Quarry after all. They would persevere with the problem of locating slate with a good bate. As usually happened with the Mandall Company, their luck was in and their perseverance proved successful. They found ample supplies at the High Blue open quarry and worked it continuously for another 40 years.

In 1924, after 43 years service to the Buttermere Company, Bennett Johns retired from the Honister quarry and returned to Coniston. This was not the end of his slate quarrying activities however. With a handful of local men he worked Goats Crag Quarry above Yewdale in a traditional manner. But it didn't last for long. By the end of the decade he had become too old to carry on and Goats Crag had closed.

When the First World War commenced, slate was classified as 'non-essential' and quarry men of fighting age went into the forces or to the munitions factories. The quarries had to contend with just ticking over. A dramatic revival in the fortunes of the industry came in 1918/1919 with the price of slate soaring to more than twice the pre-war period. This sudden improvement in trading created its own problems. Men were slow to return. Some of those who had survived the horrors in the fields of France and Belgium now had a fresh outlook on their life. There was a tremendous shortage of labour and it took at least a year for the industry to get back into full production.

Some of the quarries suffered seriously from the effect of the war and the lack of skilled men to keep them open. Some closed, some nearly closed, others managed to keep going and make the most of the latest mini-boom. The years immediately after the end of the war saw Mandalls still leading the way with their mechanisation. The Buttermere Company were beginning to be well established and the huge Hodge Close complex was on the verge of closing completely.

There was a feeling amongst some in Coniston that slate deposits in the area were almost exhausted and the industry was on its last legs. These were unfounded opinions, but understandable. For once the demand was there, but the industry could not meet it. Certainly no one would have dared to predict the major new developments that would occur within the next fifty years, on Broughton Moor and at Brossen Stone.

Difficult Times at Hodge Close

The Tilberthwaite Green Slate Company operated the Hodge Close complex of open and underground quarries. The proprietor was Mr J J Thomas, a capable manager of Welsh origin. Hodge Close suffered badly at the outbreak of the Great War. Most of the workforce was of fighting age and left for war service. The few that remained were not in sufficient numbers to continue working the quarry. But

Hodge Close, like all the Tilberthwaite quarries that had been 'open-topped', required constant attention. Falls of rock from the sides of the pits were a way of life. Unless they could be dealt with at once, the quarry floors soon became rubbished-up. If care was not taken, machinery could be damaged or even lost completely. By 1915 Hodge Close was over 300ft deep, a formidable depth for such a narrow slate band.

Production from Hodge Close ceased in September 1915. Pumping was suspended and eventually the water level rose by about 100ft. The few people who were left were moved to the nearby Peat Field and Calf How Quarries which were in the process of being developed.

During the next two years a limited amount of care and maintenance was carried out at the main quarry but in the end the inevitable happened. Early on the morning of the 19th April 1918 an enormous fall of rock occurred on the west side of the quarry. The debris from the fall was scattered over the galleries, burying the working faces in rubbish, and destroying a considerable amount of plant including a boiler, several pumps and a turbine. But worst of all was the damage to the landing platform onto which blocks from the aerial hoist were deposited. Very little was left of the platform and this, effectively, meant that the aerial hoist could no longer be used.

The hoist was essential for lifting slate clog from the quarry floor and from the galleries to the top of the quarry. The hoist consisted of a taut, horizontal wire rope suspended across the open pit. Along the rope ran a travelling cradle fitted with a block and tackle. From the cradle a haulage rope descended to the quarry floor. The cradle could move along the rope and, as the clog was lifted, the cradle would travel to the edge of the quarry pit where a platform had been constructed. The block was then lowered onto rail bogies at the platform. This type of aerial hoist was generally referred to as a 'blondin' after the famous tight rope walker of that name.

Mr Thomas immediately started considering alternative methods for dealing with the water and also for hoisting. By now there were clear signs that the war was nearly over and, with peace, the men would return and it would be important to prepare the quarry for a return to work.

The first scheme to be considered was that of driving a tunnel from lower down the hillside towards the quarry. The plan was that it would break out at the base of the pit. However after careful surveying it was found that the quarry floor was well below the lowest point in the valley and consequently the plan was abandoned. The next proposal was to call in a quarry engineering consultant. He recommended the use of powerful electric pumps and hoists but sadly the cost was much greater than the Tilberthwaite Company could afford. The quarry was already extremely deep. Although the slate bed, which was nearly vertical at this point, was obviously not deteriorating as the depth increased, the Company was

Winter weather could halt operations at the quarries for many weeks. The notable snowfalls during the winters of 1939 and 1940 halted operations at many Lake District sites. In this photograph quarrymen clear the entrance to the Middle Moss Head level on Coniston Old Man. Included in the group are Ernie Major, Bill Whelan (Snr), John Hudson, Jim Grant, Jim Cooper, Mick Jones and Frank Cooper.

Photo – Maureen Fleming

not optimistic about the future; and no doubt the Honister lads were eagerly waiting in the wings! The Buttermere Company, who operated at Honister, had control of most of the surrounding workings and were keen to take over Hodge Close as well.

Mr Thomas wrote to Mr Wadham, agent at the Buccleuch Estate. *"We are still most anxious to continue operations but in the event of our not succeeding in finding further profitable slate beds, or the feasibility of re-opening Hodge Close on a profitable basis, we would very respectively ask you if you would give us the opportunity of terminating the lease at the end of 1922 and leaving Hodge Close pit as it now stands. The narrowness of the vein and the great depth of the pit makes it extremely dangerous to work and the fall of rock at what was thought to be the abundant part of the side where our plant was placed gives us a feeling of insecurity."*

The Estate allowed them to terminate the lease. The old Tilberthwaite Company had shown great courage. They had operated a difficult site and had innovated well in doing so. It was a great personal disappointment to Mr Thomas who had worked Hodge Close for nearly 35 years.

It wasn't long before the Buttermere Company stepped in with fresh enthusiasm. New pumps were installed, the aerial hoist re-aligned and re-commissioned. Their plan was not to work the band to any greater depth but to prospect along the line of the band. The Company already worked the adjacent Parrock Quarry and, consequently, there was no problem in working the Hodge Close pit right up to and through the Parrock boundary. At the opposite (south) end of the pit the Company drove a new deep level along the band which was opened out and worked as a closehead. Another underground chamber was worked with some success on the east side.

Buttermere worked Hodge Close for nearly 35 years. They also worked the satellite quarries of Peat Field and Calf How in the woods below Holme Ground cottages. The inaccessibility of these workings created problems for the Company and eventually they constructed a short rail line from the riving area through the woods to the quarry banks. This became known as the 'Calf How Cutting', although most of the route was actually on an embankment.

Until 1946 most of the processing at Hodge Close was carried out in riving sheds on the extensive spoil bank to the west of the main quarry. After the Second World War the sheds were demolished and replaced by an ex-forces corrugated building, reputed to have once been an aircraft hangar. All the processing including sawing was carried out in this shed. The shed survived for many years after the quarry closed in the 1950s, eventually succumbing to the winter weather.

Another building which survived for several years after closure of the quarry was the quarry chapel. Within living memory the chapel was used for services once a month with the vicar of Brathay officiating. There was a sizable community within the area and the chapel was also used as a social centre, with whist drives held monthly. Sadly, during recent times, the building has been vandalised and is now completely derelict.

Mandall's Ropeways

The Mandall Company was going from strength to strength. It seemed they could do no wrong. During the early years of the present century they were working and developing their big quarries on Coniston Old Man at Moss Head, Fisher Bank, Saddlestone and Low Bank. Despite its high location, Low Water continued to provide a small but useful contribution as well. By now vertical shafts and rises linked many of the closeheads, improving ventilation and assisting in the working of the rock. Some of the closeheads were beginning to develop into extremely large chambers.

In this situation many companies would have sat back and enjoyed the fruits of their capital investment. But Mandalls were not like that. At the turn of the century they embarked on yet another major development. Between Low Bank at the bottom and Scald Cop at the top, most of the silver-grey band up the north east flank of the mountain was, by now, being actively worked. However there was one area that had still not been tried between the Moss Head workings and the ancient worked-out closeheads of Scald Cop. Here the band had not been exploited at all. It was almost certain that extensive deposits of silver-grey slate were awaiting discovery. Mandalls decided to follow their previous technique of driving a level through barren ground to intersect the band at an angle. On this occasion it was decided that the angle at which the level would be driven in relation to the band would be even more acute than before. The level would be started quite some distance round the shoulder of the mountain thereby avoiding tipped-spoil interfering with slate workings below.

During the last few weeks of the old century an inclined causeway was constructed from the existing Moss Head bank. It ran round the mountain for about 150 yards to the point 80 feet higher than Moss Head. Here work on the new level was to commence. The causeway ran beneath the old Scald Cop tips. It is very likely that some of the material in the tips was used in its construction. When completed the Company was able to bring into place all the equipment that was needed for the development of the new level.

Work on level-driving commenced during the Boer War. The level was christened Spion Kop by those working on it after the disastrous defeat of General Buller in the war in January 1900. There are other instances in mining history of developments such as this being named after particularly bloody battles. One might say that it was a reflection of the condition that the men had to suffer in the mines, but probably there was a big degree of sarcasm as well.

This photograph was taken at Hodge Close in March 1936. Percy Rawes, the quarry foreman (on left), and an assistant manoeuvre a slate tub into position as it is being lowered by the blondin crane onto the track. The tub has been hoisted from a lower part of the quarry to the right. Tubs loaded with slate were then taken through the interconnecting tunnel to the Parrock Quarry and out via the Parrock Incline. The photograph below shows the battery operated loco about to enter the interconnecting tunnel.

The blondin crane was first installed in the 1920s to hoist slate from the bottom of the quarry, as the workings went to a greater depth. Initially it was suspended in an east-west configuration below the quarry rim, secured onto the rock face. Subsequently the crane was repositioned much higher, secured to two pylons set a little way back from the rim. Ultimately the crane was re-aligned in a north-south configuration, again from pylons. It is said that the workings closed in the 1950s because the Company could not afford the cost of a new blondin rope.

Photos – Mrs M E Rawes

By 1902 the new Spion Kop level had intersected the slate band. The slate appeared to have excellent 'bate'. It seemed very likely that this would be yet another successful development. In an odd way this further success was to create problems for the Company. It meant that they had to sort out once and for all the tricky problem of transporting product from their quarries down the Old Man to Coniston station.

There were two options open to them. They could adopt the Welsh technique and construct a narrow gauge mineral line from their workings to the village. The route would include several sections of steep counterbalanced incline. The second option was to use aerial haulage.

A survey was carried out on the first option but it was ruled out because of the cost and complexity of operation. This only left the second option, there was no other alternative.

In 1902 a company specialising in aerial ropeways (The Ropeway Syndicate) was called in and was asked to quote for the construction of a system. The initial specification was for a ropeway from Spion Kop to Stubthwaite Moss. But there would be an option to extend it later right down to Coniston village. Mandalls accepted the quote and ordered the work to be done.

Stubthwaite Moss is a small marshy depression which is beneath the steep north east flank of Coniston Old Man and above the enclosed intake land. When one looks at it today it is not easy to believe that the Moss was once a hive of activity with a well graded cart road leading to it and extensive stocks of slate waiting onward shipment down to Coniston station.

The construction and commissioning of the ropeway was rapid. It consisted of nine pylons built of timber set into a stone base. Two static steel cables of 1½" diameter were suspended on the pylons. The cables were pulled taut and then firmly anchored at the bottom into beds of concrete and, at the other end, to steel pins driven into the crag at Spion Kop. A carrying cradle ran on each of the two cables. These were flat wooden structures that were linked to each other by a wire rope that ran round a sheathed wheel at the top. Operation was simple but effective. The cradle at the top was loaded with slate as the one at the bottom was being unloaded. When all was ready the brake was released and the loaded cradle descended, pulling the empty one up the other side.

The ropeway considerably improved the transport of 'made' slates down the mountain from the quarries. Proposals were considered to continue the ropeway from Stubthwaite Moss to Coniston village. The planned route was to be round the hill known locally as the Scrow, and down beside Mealy Gill to the railway. The Furness Railway Company had purchased a narrow strip of land on the high side of their Copperhouse trackbed near to Mealy Gill Bridge. This would allow additional sidings and space for a slate wharf. The proposals were not

This photograph was taken in about 1908 and shows the deep confines of the Parrock Quarry. Parrock was always a dark and sombre place but produced significant quantities of good quality light green slate with excellent bate.

The origins of Parrock go back to the early 1800s when a level was driven from the north and intersected a band of slate after about 500ft. This was worked as a closehead and in about 1850 a second lower level was driven from further down the hillside towards the valley bottom. This second level was about 1100ft long and allowed much better access for tipping.

During the first few months of 1898 the roof was removed from the closehead creating an open pit.

In this photograph the rail tracks leading to the exit level are still in place but the powered incline which transported material up to the quarry rim has yet to be constructed.

Both the levels described above still exist but access into the base of the pit is now well and truly blocked.

Photo – Mrs M E Rawes

We believe that this incline at Parrock Quarry was constructed in the years immediately prior to the Great War. It was a powered incline, with a winding drum at the incline-head operated by a steam engine. By the time the incline was constructed the quarry had been worked extensively to the north, creating a much bigger pit which was of sufficient length for the incline to be installed.

In this photograph the carrier appears to be at the head of the incline.

Very little remains today of the incline, although it is still possible to pick out its former location and part of the carrier still lies rusting in the undergrowth.

Photo provided by A Cameron

A Coniston quarryman despatches a clog of light green slate down the aerial flight from Mandall's High Blue Quarry to the Bonsor Mill, Coniston Coppermines. The date is October 1938 and the following year High Blue closed and the small workforce were transferred over to the Old Man Quarries.

Some years earlier, in 1925, the Mandall Company took over the old mine pelton wheel and compressor at the Bonsor Mill for a sum of £1 a year. They constructed a processing shed and installed an electric saw. Slate from High Blue was processed there until 1939.

The Blue Quarry aerial flight was one of five ropeways installed and operated by the Mandall Company linking their quarries with the road head. Other means of transport were considered including narrow gauge rail lines and counterbalanced inclines, but were eventually discounted. Clearly the ropeways were the best bet bearing in mind the method of operation and the terrain.   *Photo – Mike Brownlee*

implemented and the bottom terminus of the ropeway remained at Stubthwaite Moss until it was abandoned in the 1940s.

Spion Kop was not the only quarry to make use of the new ropeway. The isolated working at Low Moss Head was beginning to expand but there was no suitable means of carrying slate from there by cart. It was decided therefore to lay a narrow gauge railway track across the mountainside from the quarry to a point directly under the line of the ropeway. When slate from Low Moss Head was to be carried, the ropeway would be halted when the empty cradle travelling up the ropeway was directly over the end of the rail track. Slate would then be loaded onto it. In effect this meant that both cradles were of the same weight. The method used to get the ropeway cradles to reach their respective termini is not certain. Perhaps the ropeway was cranked by hand to allow the carriers to complete their journeys.

The Spion Kop ropeway was the first of several gravity aerial flights to operate in the Coniston fells. Mandalls would use this method of transport more and more as the years went by. In total, five ropeways would be built and commissioned at various times during the next fifty years. Clearly it was the most effective method of carrying material from such a steep and isolated location. The Spion Kop ropeway carried 'made' slates but the later ones all carried slate clog down to the processing areas. Ropeways have been used in other parts of the Lake District, in particular at Honister where an equally spectacular installation carried slate clog from a terminus half way up Honister Crag to the processing sheds at Honister Hause.

It is not proposed to describe all Mandall's ropeways in detail. Only a summary is given here.

i) SADDLESTONE ROPEWAY

Shortly after the Spion Kop ropeway had been proved successful a short one was commissioned running from the upper workings at Saddlestone down to the main bank. This ropeway was designed to carry slate clog down to the newly installed electric saw on the main bank.

ii) BRANDY CRAG ROPEWAY

For a short period slate clog from Saddlestone was riven and dressed at a small working lower down the hillside. A ropeway was installed to transport blocks down to this temporary processing point which was known as Brandy Crag. Mandalls had recently improved road access to the Brandy Crag bank. It was much easier to carry slate away by horse and cart from here than from Saddlestone above. Eventually the road to Saddlestone was re-aligned and improved to the extent that the dressing of slate at Brandy Crag became unnecessary and the ropeway was abandoned.

iii) Blue Quarries Ropeway

During the 1920s the fortunes of Blue Quarries above Coppermines Valley changed very much for the better. Mandalls had at last found an excellent area of light green slate with a good 'bate' at High Blue Quarry. A cart road had been constructed to High Blue but, with the final closure of the Coniston Mine, it was decided to build an aerial flight linking High Blue with the old Bonsor Dressing Floor where once copper ore had been processed. The ropeway had, in total, three pylons and operated successfully for about fifteen years until the Blue Quarry workings closed at the start of the Second World War. An electrically driven saw was set up at the Coppermines to cut slate blocks prior to riving.

iv) Moss Head Ropeway

The fifth and final ropeway at Coniston was constructed just prior to the Second War. It ran from the Moss Head workings to the main bank at Saddlestone, a vertical height of about 500ft. This ropeway was of a much more up to date design than the previous ones. Remains of it lie abandoned on the mountainside. A few years after it was commissioned several of the pylons were replaced by second hand ones purchased from the Honister Quarries. Near Fisher Bank a toppled pylon lies on its side and the main carrying cables and haulage ropes are strewn up the hillside.

There were two reasons for constructing the Moss Head Ropeway. The first was that the cart road down from Moss Head to Saddlestone was becoming increasingly difficult to keep open because it was being encroached upon by tippings from above. Secondly, within the mountain, the working chambers were becoming a colossal size. The workings in the roof of High Moss Head had broken through the floor of Spion Kop in two places. Similarly the working of the roof of Middle Moss Head had caused it to break through the floor of High Moss Head. Consequently all the various closeheads in this area were rapidly becoming one huge void.

Because the closeheads were beginning to join up underground, Spion Kop was soon to cease to be a separate undertaking. Slate clog from there would be lowered down to the Moss Head closehead and be brought out via the Moss Head level. Effectively this sounded the death-knell for slate dressing on the Spion Kop bank, for the Spion Kop ropeway and also for the stock yard on Stubthwaite Moss.

The closure of the Spion Kop ropeway marked the end of an era. The rattling of the cradles as they moved up and down became so familiar to fell walkers and those following the hunt that they ceased to notice them. At the time of writing this book there are a few veteran hunt followers and fell walkers around who can still remember the ropeway in operation, with the cradles laden with dressed slate slowly inching their way down the mountainside.

A low winter's sun creates long shadows across the fellside above the Coppermines Valley. For at least 300 years slate has been worked at Blue Quarry. The last area worked was High Blue, just below the skyline. Despite its name the colour of the slate obtained from these quarries was green. In this photograph, which was taken from the Saddlestone Bank on Coniston Old Man, the various roads and tracks serving Blue Quarry can be seen very clearly.

Also visible in the photograph is a much earlier road which can still be followed. To the right of the quarries are the 'tight' zigzags of an old 'peat-road' which was probably in use well before the 17th Century for bringing peat down from the Kitty Crag peat-moss, one of Coniston's most productive mosses. Peat was being cut at Kitty Crag long before Blue Quarries were even thought of.

Peat mosses on the high fells and commons above Coniston developed as a result of extensive felling of timber during the Bronze Age. Although this prehistoric act was environmentally extremely damaging, it provided an alternative fuel for Coniston dwellings during the Middle Ages, a time when all felled timber was in great demand for charcoal production.

Photo – A Cameron

Generating power for Mandalls Quarries

As well as improving the transport of slate the other pressing requirement of the Mandall Company as it expanded was to provide electricity and compressed air for its various workings. Compressed air was needed to operate the rock drills, several pneumatic hoists and also the air operated winches which were being used to lift slate clog onto rail trucks or the ropeway carriers. Electricity was required for the electric saws and also, subsequently, to provide lighting for the underground workings.

There were two power sources used at the Old Man Quarries. The first was at the Smithy below the Saddlestone tip. It was fed by a pipe from Low Water Tarn which provided water for a Schram Harker pelton wheel. The pelton wheel, which is a form of turbine, drove a twin cylinder single stage air compressor and also an electricity generator. Within the Power House was an air receiver which delivered air by compressed-air pipes to all the working levels on this side of the Old Man. This unit was only just sufficient for their needs and as more air operated winches were installed, it began to have great difficulty in coping with the demand.

The second source of power was at the Bonsor Mill in the Coppermines Valley. Here the old compressor, which had once been used to provide power for the Coniston Mine, was still more or less in working order. This unit was also based on a pelton wheel which was driven by water piped down the fellside from a series of water leats above. Mandalls took over the unit in 1925 for the sum of £1 a year, which, even in those days, must have been considered a bargain. A compressed air pipe was laid up the fellside to the Smithy at Saddlestone where it was coupled into the air receiver.

Bob Taylforth, who lived in Miner's Row in the Coppermines Valley, had the job of operating the compressor. His first task early in the morning was to lubricate the compressor and pelton wheel bearings. The pelton wheel was 'locked' during the night to prevent it rotating. This was done by jamming a steel rod through the spokes of the wheel. Bob would then climb up the fellside to open the sluice gate in the water race. This would fill the down-pipe with water. He would then return to the valley to start the pelton wheel. The reverse procedure was adopted in the evening. At a later date the operation of the compressor became the responsibility of Bert Smith.

The Bonsor Mill plant was also used to provide compressed air and electricity to the Blue Quarries. A building was constructed close to the power plant in which slate clog from High Blue was sawn. When Blue Quarry closed in 1939 the compressor was again taken out of commission but was later used by the Lakeland Green Slate and Stone Company.

Don Kelly, who now works at Elterwater Quarries, remembers the daily routine at the Old Man Quarries. "*In the morning I used to go up to the Smithy and put the water on to the electrics. I would turn the pelton wheel off at night but we would leave the pipe running to take the pressure off it. If you didn't it was very prone to leaking. We used to turn the tarn off at night if we were short of water. If we had turned it off, Ray Cluett used go up there first thing in the morning to turn it back on again."*

In more recent times power was supplied by diesel powered generators and compressors. But during these earlier years it was a credit to the quarrymen that they were able to operate with power derived from the natural elements for so long.

Bert Smith, quarry engineer

Bert started work at the Coniston quarries soon after completing his engineering apprenticeship in 1938. Eventually he became responsible for the operation of the Coppermines compressor and also the equipment in the smithy below Smithy Bank on the Old Man. He also had to attend to all the equipment on the quarry banks and within the closeheads when there was a break-down. Despite a demanding workload he managed to keep the site running, often against all odds.

Bert's other skill was as a craftsman builder of violins. The instruments he built were of such high quality that, eventually, he decided to quit his job on the Old Man and concentrate on making violins. Clearly this was his forté and he converted the loft in his house in Tilberthwaite Avenue to a workshop, travelled to the Alps to purchase specialist woods and produce instruments which were much in demand. His skills became internationally accepted but he never made more than four instruments a year, although he could have sold many more.

Bert died in 1973. His widow still has a letter written shortly after his death which reads as follows:

Dear Mrs Smith

I was heartbroken to learn of your dear husband's death. I shall never forget the wonderful visit I had with him in his workshop in Coniston. Though it was in the glare of television lights I was so absorbed and fascinated in his work that I believe we were both oblivious of the BBC.

Please accept my deepest sympathy.

Yehudi Menuin

Photo provided by Mrs Bert Smith, source unknown

THE CANN STORY

The story of this remarkable family actually starts towards the end of the nineteenth century at a time when new names and strange accents began to be evident in the Lake District. Because of a serious depression in the slate industry elsewhere, in particular in Wales and Cornwall, many skilled slate workers moved to the area to seek work. It must have seemed to them, from a distance, that Furness and Lakeland were a minor 'El Dorado'. Large numbers moved north finding employment in the iron ore mines in Low Furness and the slate quarries on the fells.

We can get an interesting indication from old records of where they settled. Many went to the Hodbarrow iron ore mine at Millom on the Cumbrian coast. A few found work in the Coniston and Tilberthwaite Copper Mines although the Coniston Mine was in a state of serious decline at that time. Many from the Delabole slate quarry on the north Cornish coast found employment in the slate quarries at Honister, Elterwater and, in particular, at Coniston. One family who moved to Coniston was to have a greater effect on the future fortunes of the village than any other.

Claude Cann was 12 years old when his father left Delabole in 1890 and came north to look for work. After a short time in the slate quarries on Coniston Old Man he moved to Hodbarrow. Claude grew up to be an exceptionally resourceful and talented young man. His father offered to support him in any apprenticeship he cared to choose but, even at the age of 13, he knew what he wanted to do. He would follow in his father's footsteps and be a slate quarryman. His greatest ambition was to operate his own quarry and by the age of 26 his ambition was realised. With a number of colleagues he had carried out successful trials at a small outcrop working on the hillside above the Tilberthwaite Valley. There they had found good rock with excellent 'bate'. The working was opened up enthusiastically. This was the beginning of the High Fellside Quarry.

High Fellside was very successful, so much so that, in 1910, the Buttermere Green Slate Company made Claude an offer for it as a going concern which he accepted. He was retained as manager, a position he held until the outbreak of the Great War.

At the onset of the war Claude was posted to the Yarlside Iron Ore Mines at Barrow in Furness which was considered to be work of national importance. His position at High Fellside was kept open and at the end of the war the Company wrote to him three times asking him to return. He could see no prospects however other than being an ordinary quarryman under the eyes of Buttermere Green Slate Company. This was not what he wanted, although he had shares in the Buttermere

Company, he felt it was time to have a change. He refused the offer and took up the tenancy of Outrake Farm at Park Gate, a mile south of Coniston village.

Outrake was an old, established, traditional hill farm with some arable land. It had once, coincidentally, been the registered office of the Cove and Banniside Slate Company. Claude farmed it for six years. He also established a carting business and employed a number of local men to carry slate down from the high quarries. One of these was Harold Grisedale who frequently carried slate down from the Torver quarries. Harold had the distinction of carting the last load of slate down from the remote quarry at Ash Gill at the time of its closure in the 1920s. The proprietor of Ash Gill at the time was Casson Brockbank who is reputed to have lived by himself up at these lonely workings.

Farming at Outrake also allowed Claude time to think and plan ahead and also to build up an acquaintance with two men who were to feature strongly in his life for the next few years.

James O'Mara was a quarryman who originated from Coniston. Henry Mellon came from Kirkby-in-Furness and was a mining engineer. Along with Claude Cann they decided, in 1925, to set up a Company to quarry slate. Their initial plan was to work the Gold Scope Quarry on Brown Pike but the lease holder was not prepared to relinquish the lease and the group eventually decided to work slate on Broughton Moor above Torver. This is a desolate place even in the summer months. A number of small workings had been started during the 1800s. In 1919 Mr Mellon had taken up the lease for quarrying slate there from the Broughton Tower Estates, initially for a period of 14 years. The rent was £20 a year. He had worked the Lag Bank Quarry in this area. It had not been a huge success. Claude had spent some time studying the dip and rise of the slate courses and he had come to the conclusion that at Broughton Moor these were altogether different from those found elsewhere. He was absolutely convinced that extensive areas of slate were there to be won, if only they could be located.

The group decided to continue working Lag Bank while they prospected on other parts of Broughton Moor. During this time they drove the Tail Adit and obtained some useable slate. Meanwhile Claude completed his study of the lie of the slate beds and put his plans to his two colleagues. Because of the nature of the strata he recommended driving a dip tunnel from a point some distance below Lag Bank. Henry Mellon was thoroughly unconvinced. More than once he had been recommended by local quarrymen to drive an adit in a particular direction only to find nothing there. Now his colleague was recommending driving a dip tunnel. In the end Claude Cann's persuasion won and in 1928 the level was started. Work progressed for many months and eventually the level entered an area of slate rock of massive formation but unfortunately it was totally unsuitable for riving as the cleavage was twisted and the rock fractured. The drive was abandoned, most of the available capital had been used up and the partners called a meeting.

This short length of incline is situated within the Spion Kop workings on Coniston Old Man. It was constructed to allow slate clogs to be collected from the closehead at the head of the incline to start the journey out of the mountain. The incline was powered by a small air winch. More recently the Moss Head workings directly beneath broke into Spion Kop from below, just to the left of the photograph. In the roof approximately directly above the photographer's head, a narrow shaft or 'smoke hole' was driven leading up to the Scald Cop workings high above.

Photo – Jon Knowles

At the meeting Claude obviously had his back to the wall. Henry Mellon refused to put another penny into the concern. He was beginning to find Claude Cann very irritating. James O'Mara had borrowed heavily from his wife's uncle and was badly in debt. But Claude was convinced that, if only they could keep going, they would be successful. He was even prepared to back his own conviction and pay the wages of the men out of his own bank account for a few months. The other two could not disagree with this and work started again on Claude's dip tunnel, driving it on through the area of fractured rock. After a further 18 feet the men struck a fault. It ran at right angles to the direction of the slate bed. They drove on through the fault. Beyond it was a vast area of high quality slate. Claude's convictions had been justified. He had found it at last.

Extraction of the rock began immediately. From less than a dozen men in 1928 the quarry grew rapidly in size so that, ten years later, over 100 men were employed. Initially Broughton Moor was worked entirely as an underground quarry but eventually a start was made to remove the roofs of some of the closeheads and the quarry reverted to a classic 'pit and terrace working' as is found in several areas of Snowdonia. The open pits were accessed by tunnels which served each of the terraces in the pit. As the years progressed Claude Cann continued to show innovative flair. He introduced diamond sawing equipment and also the concept of wire sawing of the face, a practice which he had seen at the Carrara marble quarries in Italy. When used to cut across the bate a diamond saw will give a much better splitting edge to a block and increase the number of slates that a river can produce in a given time. He also perfected the 'heading blast' whereby explosives are packed at the back of a face to be removed, reached by tunnels. The base of the face is then cut completely through with a wire saw. When the explosives are detonated the face is pushed outwards, broken into massive blocks which are then removed from the quarry floor.

Within a few years of the expansion starting Henry Mellon sold his share of the concern to Mr E P Brown, the managing director of the Carrs Biscuit Company of Carlisle. Henry and Claude had never really 'hit it off' from the start. In reality there were probably faults on both sides. Claude found Henry cautious and un-dynamic and more than once Henry accused Claude of being far too ambitious.

The sale of Henry Mellon's shares created problems for Claude. Mr Brown now owned 51% of the share holding and was determined to enforce his authority as the major share-holder. This did not suit Claude at all and many wrangles ensued. Eventually the Cann family managed to buy out Mr Brown's share and Broughton Moor eventually came under the complete control of the one family.

In 1932 Claude's son, Arthur, joined the Company. Arthur had been born in 1907, attended Ulverston Grammar School and then worked for nine years at Carrs Biscuit Company. While at Carrs he had taken his articles and qualified as a cost accountant. It was Mr Brown's suggestion that Arthur should move to Broughton Moor. Because of the rapid expansion his father was not able to keep tabs on all aspects of the operation. He was also well into his fifties.

Arthur had a very positive effect on the fortunes of Broughton Moor. While Claude concentrated on innovation in the manufacturing operation, Arthur was able to expand the customer base. It was an ideal team. Broughton Moor rapidly became the leading quarry company in the Coniston area. At first he didn't find it easy. He was not a born salesman but eventually he started to win orders and then, according to the men at the quarry, he 'didn't look back'.

As the quarry expanded so the workforce increased. Many of the men travelled from Low Furness to Torver on the train and were then driven by the quarry lorry up to Broughton Moor. At the same time many men from Coniston and Torver were travelling daily down the railway to work in the steelworks and the shipyard in Barrow. The railway was essential, the lifeline of the community.

The late Tommy Gregg, a quarryman from Coniston, remembered well the years before the Second World War. Tommy started work at Broughton Moor in 1936. The moor itself was very much a grouse moor and he remembers the ground *"thick with them, and their chicks."* In those days all the workings, with the exception of one, were underground. As the Company purchased larger machines he can remember the closehead roofs being removed one by one and eventually all the active workings were 'open-top'.

Tommy served time as a dresser along with another apprentice, Ike Walker of Torver. When the war started many of the younger men left their employment to fight for their country. Only the older ones remained to work the quarry. There was little requirement for roofing slates during the war years and he can remember them stacked 'nearly up to heaven' on the quarry bank. But soon another market opened up. Understandably the demand for monumental work increased and eventually Tommy retrained as an engraver and spent the remainder of his time with the Company carrying out the skilled job of lettering memorial stones.

"Broughton Moor was a great place to work, everybody was local and everybody was friendly. We had a great many laughs. For some time Jim O'Mara was the boss. He was living in Barrow but moved into the old mill house directly opposite Coniston Catholic Church. His son Bernie became the postman. Men used to be collected from as far away as Millom and taken by wagon up to Broughton Moor, and back home again in the evenings.

"After the war we started to produce more and more cladding for buildings. But that only came about with the introduction of modern machinery from Italy. Had we had the machines before the war a lot of stone could have been used which ended up on the tip. Some of the tips up on Coniston Old Man contain thousands of tons which could be used now."

69

We believe that this Anderson Grice saw was located on the Middle Bank at Broughton Moor and that the photograph was taken about 60 years ago, at a time when health and safety precautions were of little concern.

Photo – CATMHS Archives, source unknown

Broughton Moor opened offices at Wraysdale House close to the centre of Coniston village. Subsequently the same offices were used by Burlington Slate for a number of years after they took over the Broughton Moor Company.

It was in the years after the war that the Company started noticing that the slate market was changing. In 1958 Claude Cann, in a talk he gave to the Ambleside Field Sports Society, commented that: "*during the last few months there has been a recession in the slate trade. The main reason for this is the very keen and acute competition by roofing tiles which can be placed on a roof at little over a third of the cost of Westmoreland Green Slate. Another reason is that a younger generation of architects has come on the scene. At the outbreak of the last war we had thirteen school contracts on our books, each of which was calling for, approximately, between forty and a hundred tons of roofing material. Today we have not one school on our books for roofing slates, and it is hardly likely that the younger generation of architects will revert to specifications which they consider to be antiquated. However, to off-set this we are enjoying an excellent demand for slabs for facing large and important buildings in various towns and cities.*"

To keep up with these trends the Company, in the 1950s and '60s, continued to implement modern techniques on an impressive scale. It was important to turn over a high tonnage of material quickly to keep the market price of the finished product competitive. There was abundant raw material in the form of slate rock with excellent bate. Because of this there was little concern to limit the wastage caused by blasting which was often in the region of 90%. It was far more important, in fact, to work the face using a minimum quantity of powder and man hours, both of which were expensive commodities. Because of this the heading blast technique was used frequently. Such a blast could bring down over a quarter of a million tons of rock in one go, and with less powder than conventional methods. Nowadays there is much more concern to reduce wastage as much as possible. This is not just for environmental reasons, but waste rock has to be dumped somewhere and that can cause problems with planning authorities.

In 1957 the Company decided to expand by taking over the operation of the Elterwater Green Slate Company from the Mors Moler concern. Elterwater Quarry had a long history. Slate was first extracted there in the 1700s and, in 1898 the workings had been taken over by the Buttermere Green Slate Company whose main operating site was at Honister. In recent years the Honister concern had found it necessary to close several of their quarries, and Elterwater had ceased to operate in 1952. But Elterwater's light green slate was very much in demand and in three years the quarry was working again. In 1957 Broughton Moor also purchased the mineral rights for the nearby Spout Crag Quarry situated in woodland on the steep southern slopes of the Langdale Valley. A road was constructed from Spout Crag to Elterwater. All slate extracted from Spout Crag was taken to the sawing sheds at Elterwater for processing.

The Company was innovating constantly. In 1960 the decision was taken to convert the remaining underground workings at Broughton Moor to open-top operation. The closehead roofs were taken off over a period of time and several chambers were joined up. All quarrying was then carried out in open pits which were accessed by levels running in from the main banks. Wire sawing, which had been used to a small extent for many years, was also introduced extensively during the 1960s. Unlike the modern diamond-wire saws of today, these relatively crude installations used silica sand as the cutting agent. However, at that time, they were a major step forward and allowed the quarrymen to cut through the faces which were due to be blasted thus reducing the wastage by localising the shatter of the blast and also reducing the amount of powder required to do the work.

The Company were proud that they were in the forefront of processing technology. At any one time they were constantly evaluating new equipment and techniques. A number of masonry sheds were in use at the quarry and these contained much state-of-the-art equipment. There was also a quite extensive maintenance workshop on the No 2 Bank.

It wasn't just their main quarry that benefited from capital investment. A considerable amount of money was invested in the Elterwater Quarry as well. In the mid 1960s the old processing sheds were enlarged and a new splitting shed was built. At the same time a smart new office building was also completed which included a drawing office and reception area.

In March 1966 the Broughton Moor Company acquired the mineral rights to the Brathay Slab Quarry which had been out of operation for a number of years. Three months later they started production. The quarry is situated in woodland to the north of Hawkshead. It produced a slate that was virtually black and, on polishing, would give an outstanding finish. There was still abundant slate at Brathay and the nature of the rock was such that blocks of a massive size could be obtained. In fact within a few months of it re-opening, the quarry was producing at a rate of 400 tons a month with a labour force of only four men. All the sawing was carried out at either Broughton Moor or Elterwater.

Brathay slate was remarkable, both in appearance and size. In their sales literature the Company was able to promote slabs which were 8ft x 3½ft x 1" thick and also 'altar slabs' up to 12ft long.

Broughton Moor was developing an extensive product portfolio. By now the emphasis was almost entirely on architectural slate. At the beginning of 1968 the total work force was 135 with about 40 of them at Elterwater. A few years earlier Harold Ogden had become sales manager. He had joined the firm in 1950 and was now to expand the overseas market considerably. Harold began to travel extensively, making a point of seeing his European customers at least once a year. The UK sales force was also re-organised and agents were set up in a number of centres. It seemed that nothing could stop the Company under the guidance of the

72

Cann family. During the 1950s and '60s Arthur Cann took over much more of the running of the Company. Despite his age his father continued to play his part where he could. But his health was failing and in 1968 he died, aged 90 years.

The death of Claude Cann marked the end of an era for the slate quarrying industry and also for Coniston village. If one person stands out as being responsible for the present prosperity of the community, then it must be him. Coniston people are not known for imparting folk with grand testimonials, and no memorial stands in the village to this remarkable person. But on all continents of the world countless reminders of the product of his Company stand in his honour. A few have been selected here. In the UK the National Library of Scotland contains floors, columns and staircases of slate from Broughton Moor. In London many examples exist including the Times Building which is clad in slate from the quarry. In Australia the Port Line building in Sydney (at the time it was built it was one of the tallest in the city) is also clad with slate from Broughton Moor. The National Hall in the African city of Lagos used considerable quantities of slate from both Broughton Moor and Spout Crag and in Montreal the magnificent headquarters of the Canadian Bank of Commerce is clad for all its 600ft height in slate from Spout Crag quarry. These and other contracts were to lead to the Queen's Award for Industry in 1969 for export achievements.

Claude's ability had been exceptional. He and his son had transformed the industry. There was a noticeable sense of pride in this achievement. Quarrymen working at Broughton Moor considered themselves to be the elite. To the boys in Mr Curry's class at the village school, having a dad working at Broughton Moor was the highest accolade and many left as soon as they had reached their fourteenth birthday to follow in their father's footsteps, often taking up his trade, and nickname as well.

But the death of Claude was a turning point. It marked the start of a considerable period of uncertainty for the Broughton Moor Company and its employees which was reflected throughout the area as a whole. Within two years, unknown to the workforce, the Company was put up for sale. The news broke when a buyer was found. The Delabole Company of Cornwall were to be the new owners of Broughton Moor. At that time Delabole was not felt to be a dynamic, well organised company and ownership lasted just three years. Tommy Gregg remembered this time well.

"Things seemed to go from bad to worse when Delabole took over. They were not very well organised and we seemed to have one director after another up there.

"Then they started asking for redundancies. No one knew why. The firm was in good order. We asked George Bains who was the boss at the quarry what was going on but he didn't know either. About twenty of us went for redundancy. Then we heard that Delabole were going to sell. Eventually we heard that it was

73

Lord Cavendish that was going to buy it. They had me earmarked to go to Elterwater to work. I didn't want to go there so I left. I have never been back up the hill since the day I came down."

In general there was great relief that Lord Cavendish had taken the Company over, although this was tinged with a little anxiety. He operated the huge Burlington Slate Quarry on Kirkby Moor. He also controlled a share in the Lakeland Green Slate Company who worked the highly successful Brossen Stone Quarry at Coniston which produced a very similar product to Broughton Moor. Would the Cavendish family eventually take over the whole of Lakeland? Was there room for both Brossen Stone and Broughton Moor to continue operating? The complete control of Lakeland did occur three years later in 1975 and, although the numbers working at the quarries have declined considerably in recent years, it was to be Broughton Moor and Elterwater that would continue operating more or less continuously through the 1980s and into the '90s while Bursting Stone had lengthy periods of being 'mothballed'.

One victim of the take-over by Lord Cavendish was the Brathay Slab Quarry. In 1976, just before Brathay was shut down, George Tarr worked at the quarry. *"Brathay was a good quarry at all times. There was such good rock that you didn't have one poor face. We just peeled off the lumps and stocked them on the quarry floor ready to be taken away. As soon as Burlington took over Broughton Moor they shut Brathay and just let it flood."*

Effectively the take-over of the Broughton Moor Company by Lord Cavendish marks the end of the Cann's active involvement in the running of the quarries. However members of the family still figure prominently. Arthur Cann continued to live in Coniston for a number of years until, after the death of his first wife, he re-married and moved to Scotland. He died in 2004. His elder daughter, Kathleen, was also very much involved in the industry as a member of the sales team at the Burlington Slate offices at Kirkby.

BETWEEN THE WARS

Coniston between the wars was a peaceful place. There was steady employment at the quarries despite the fact that, during the 1920s, the industry was in yet another state of depression. Slate prices had fallen sharply again. Production costs had remained high. Clearly, never again would fortunes be made by the small operators in the industry.

The industry was changing as well. There was now less emphasis on the bargain setting by Companies of men. More and more individuals would be employed by the proprietors. For a while the two systems worked alongside each other but by the late 1940s the Company structure was a thing of the past. This opened the door for quarrymen to move between proprietors much more freely until they found a quarry and workmates who suited them best.

By the end of the 1930s the number of quarries still working was a fraction of those in 1920. At Torver the Cove and Gold Scope quarries had closed down. So too had the slab quarries at Ash Gill, Banniside and Addyscale. On Coniston Old Man the Low Water Quarry had also closed as had many of the Tilberthwaite workings and also the slab quarries at Guards and at Cat Bank. But Broughton Moor was expanding and Mandalls and the Buttermere Company were still providing steady employment.

Daily life in Coniston had remained unchanged for many years. Quarrymen working at Tilberthwaite walked or cycled to work. Many lodged at Holme Ground cottages, the terrace of houses built in the wood close to Hodge Close Quarry. To reach the Old Man Quarries quarrymen walked up from Dixon Ground via Coniston Waterfall and Miner's Bridge. Tommy Gregg, who, as a small boy, lived in the Coppermines Valley remembered the men walking to work daily. *"You could see then going up in the morning in winter with their lanterns and big umbrellas – massive ones made of cane so they could knock them back when they blew out. They all used to wear large sacks to keep themselves warm. In the evenings they would all set off from the quarry and run down, just like a fell-race."*

In the mid 1920s Tommy started school in Coniston. He had to walk down from the Mines in the morning and back in the evening, frequently in the dark. Mandalls had taken over the whole of the cottages on Miner's Row for an initial rent of £16:10s a year to provide homes for quarrymen. Consequently the valley was full of young local families with children.

Mandalls had also rented the Copperhouse at the head of the railway. The intention was to use it to load slate from the Blue Quarries. Unfortunately, because of the narrowness of the dock, they could only load onto narrow, low sided wagons. Many of the trucks which carried slate were fitted with improved suspension to prevent damage to the cargo. The station master at Coniston at the time was Harold Satterthwaite. He had an extremely helpful nature and assisted the quarry proprietors greatly in arranging the shipment of their goods. He will also be remembered as someone who did a considerable amount for the village in general.

Slate from the Tilberthwaite area was carted to Coniston station via a stock yard at the side of the main Coniston to Ambleside road in Yewdale. This was situated at the entrance to the wood about 200 yards below the old limekiln. Here the full loads arriving from the quarries would be split with some of the slate removed to allow the horses to cope with the steep hill up to Coniston station.

In 1933 a small new venture was started in Tilberthwaite that would run for a number of years. It involved Coniston miner John Willie Shaw and his financial backer Oscar Gnosspelius. Both men were aware of a deposit of slate that had been found at Horse Crag in Tilberthwaite. John Willie was convinced that it could be worked profitably.

Horse Crag had had an interesting history. In 1849 John Barrett, owner of Coniston Copper Mines, approved a major development to drive a long adit in a westerly direction from a point just above the Tilberthwaite valley road. The adit, which became known as Horse Crag Level, was intended to intersect the deep workings of the Tilberthwaite Mine at the head of the Gill. It would provide a means of removing copper ore and also help in the draining of the deep mine. The adit took ten years to complete and proved to be a very costly development. In fact it probably never paid for itself. About 300ft in from the entrance the tunnel had cut through an area of good slate rock.

Shaw inspected carefully the slate in the abandoned Horse Crag Level. He felt that it would be worth mining, using the level to bring the rock out. Oscar Gnosspelius agreed to put up the necessary finance. For a number of years Shaw worked Horse Crag with two colleagues as an underground closehead. He continued working there until, in 1938, he became too old to carry on and had to retire. During the period of time a considerable quantity of slate was removed from the underground working and also from two small open-top quarries nearby, and dressed on the bank outside. At first Shaw drilled all the shot-holes by hand but eventually an old paraffin-engined air compressor was brought up to Horse Crag which allowed shot holes to be machine bored.

During the time that Shaw and Oscar Gnosspelius were involved at Horse Crag the well known writer of children's stories, Arthur Ransome, was researching his latest book, *Pigeon Post*. Ransome visited Horse Crag and as a consequence modelled his character 'Slater Bob' on John Willie and the shy 'Squashy Hat' on Oscar Gnosspelius. Much of the technical data on mining and mineral veins in the book was a result of discussions with Gnosspelius.

76

Tourism was now in full swing. Many of the large houses in the area were occupied by families who had moved to the village from the industrial areas in the south. Several of them had quite an influence on the way of life. One family which was to have a dramatic effect on the village and its history came to Coniston for the first time just prior to the start of the Second World War. Malcom Campbell arrived in the summer of 1939 to attempt to break the world water speed record on the lake. He came with a brand new boat named *Bluebird* and his visit coincided with an unusually calm spell of weather. By the time he left, just days before the outbreak of war, he had registered a new water speed record of 141.74 m.p.h. This was by no means the last visit that the Campbell family made to Coniston.

Following the hunt was as popular between the wars as it is today. Usually the hunt would visit the Old Man area twice a year, normally in February and November, and would spend up to a week there. For the men up at the quarries these were great days. When the hunt was in the vicinity the whole workforce would be out on the tip-end waiting for them. Many quarrymen would put in extra hours during the previous weeks to build up stock so that they could take time-off and join in with the hunt, often travelling as far as Langdale or Eskdale, only to have to return to the quarries before the end of the day to pick up their bag and head back down to Coniston.

Many men attended hound trail events and some kept their own trail hounds. Just prior to the Second World War Jack Taylforth and George Brownlee, two quarrymen working at Blue Quarry, planned jointly to buy a trail hound. They decided to renovate the old smithy at Blue Quarry and convert it into a kennel. One of them would come to work an hour early each day to walk the dog and the other partner would do the same in the evening. This was a very convenient arrangement for Jack and George. Unfortunately the dog didn't think so and its howling kept the residents of the Coppermines Valley awake for many nights.

Many quarrymen took their dogs to work. The animals would make themselves at home in the cabins waiting for their masters to return for their bait. A story that is still told today concerned a mongrel dog called Tony, owned by quarryman Alf Coward. Alf was a river and was based for a period of time at High Brandy Crag Quarry, where sawn clogs of slate were riven. The quarry had once been a working quarry and the level and closehead were still open. As there was little shelter on the bank in bad weather, the men would retire into the underground closehead and light a fire at bait time. If the fire had been lit previously and was still smouldering, the simplest way to bring it back to life was to throw petrol on it. Unfortunately, on the day in question, Tony was accidentally deluged in petrol which ignited. The dog fled down the level and out into the rain where the flames were put out. Fortunately it came to no harm.

Just prior to the outbreak of the war an incident occurred in Coniston which is still remembered to this day. The New Year's Honours List of 1939 brought it to the attention of the nation as a whole. Within its long list of names, was that of 'Mr George Frederick Coward, quarryman, of Coniston', who was awarded the British Empire Medal for 'leadership and courage' during a rescue of a colleague on Coniston Old Man the previous winter.

George was foreman at Mandalls. Although he had spent most of his working life at the Old Man Quarries he actually originated from Langdale. He was a particularly modest person, a keen member of Coniston bowls and cricket teams and also a bandmaster of long standing.

On 13th December 1937 heavy snow had fallen at Coniston. The roads into the village were blocked for several hours and snow continued to fall during the following night. The next day quarrymen started work at the Old Man Quarries as usual although the walk up from the village had been quite an ordeal. Snow continued to fall during the day and the wind started to increase. Conditions were clearly becoming serious and by late morning most of the men up at the high Spion Kop workings decided they should beat a retreat quickly.

Two of the younger men, Matthew Walker who lived at the Coppermines and Jim Long from Coniston village, decided to stay up at the high workings. Within the closehead at Spion Kop, conditions were relatively comfortable. There was little indication of the gale and blizzard blowing on the mountain outside. But by 2pm even these two began to realise that they should get down quickly. They didn't relish the prospect of being stranded up at Spion Kop for several days.

The track down from Spion Kop is narrow and traverses a steep slope below the ancient tips of Scald Cop. Above them snow had compacted in the high wind and a large cornice had formed. As they descended an avalanche started. A huge mass of snow swept down engulfing both of them. Matthew Walker was carried some distance down the mountainside and ended up on a small ledge. When he finally forced his way out from under the snow he realised how far he had been carried. Jim Long was nowhere to be seen.

Matthew managed to descend to the buildings on the main bank at Saddlestone. George Coward and a few other quarrymen were still there. George immediately organised a search of the mountainside below the Spion Kop track. The wind was rising all the time and the blizzard conditions were becoming much more serious. After an hour and a half of searching George called a halt and ordered the men to return to the village. He would then organise a larger search by lantern light.

At 7.30pm a large group of men assembled in the village and started the trek back up to Saddlestone. Not a single person who had been contacted failed to turn up. In Coniston wives and families gathered waiting for their return. It was optimistically felt that they might be back by midnight. By 3am most started to get worried. It was to be another three and a half hours before the rescuers returned to everyone's great relief, and were able to recount the night's events.

The group had struggled back up to Saddlestone and had lit a fire in one of the buildings. The search then commenced. Details were reported graphically in the following day's *Evening Mail*:

> "*They found that the wind and snow conditions had worsened since the afternoon, but that some moonlight was getting through. The foreman, with wisdom, so placed his men that they could take such shelter as was possible during the worst periods, and make a rapid search during the lulls.*
>
> "*Somewhere about 2.30am, after a gust of great violence, the rescuers heard an answer to their cries. Conditions were extremely bad, and there was a visibility of about nine yards only.*
>
> "*At the end of a quarter of an hour an outstretched arm was seen emerging from the snow, off which a great weight had just been lifted by the last terrific gust. With great difficulty Jim Long was carried to the lower quarry by the rescuers who were often in the snow up to their necks. During the descent the foreman continually called the roll of the party to assure himself that no one had disappeared.*
>
> "*At Saddlestone, Long was dried in front of the fire, rubbed, put into warm clothing, and given restoratives. When sufficiently recovered he was put on a stretcher and carried down the mountain, again a long and difficult matter. This last journey which is normally done by the average quarryman in twenty minutes, occupied the rescuers over three hours, the village being reached about 6.30am.*"

As one can imagine, there was great relief in the village that all had returned safely. Jim Long was an extremely lucky lad. It is very unlikely that present day mountain rescue teams would risk a search in such conditions under darkness. They would probably wait until first light. The incident clearly demonstrates the ties, loyalties and team spirit of closely knit communities such as Coniston. Jim Long returned to work in the quarries for a number of years after the war ended. George Coward was not too keen about being awarded the British Empire Medal. He felt that it should have been presented to all the men who had taken part.

THE CHANGING YEARS

The Second World War had taken its toll, not just in lives lost but also in all aspects of life including the effect on the industrial infrastructure of Britain. For the slate industry, which had been classified as 'non-essential', the end of the war brought a replay of the events of 1918. Repairs to buildings in the industrial cities created a short term demand but, this time, the boom was small and many manufacturers were not able to respond immediately. During the war a number of quarries such as Hodge Close had been mothballed. Others only just kept on working; it depended very much on the age of the workforce at the start of the war. The Broughton Moor Quarry was fortunate, production continued in a fashion and slate was stockpiled on the quarry banks.

As with the previous war, it took a few years for the industry to get back to normal, but eventually the quarries started up again at full strength. By now there had been a considerable thinning out of the industry. At Torver, only the Broughton Moor quarry was operating. Mandalls were still working at the Old Man with both the higher and lower banks in full production. At Tilberthwaite the only quarry operating was Hodge Close, worked by the Buttermere Company. Buttermere had suffered badly during the war. Their main workings at Honister and Yew Crag had been closed down completely, the efforts to keep the quarries operating had been seriously hindered by the severe snows of January 1940. The energetic Commander Hoare, proprietor of the Buttermere Company, put all his efforts into getting the Honister, Hodge Close and Elterwater operations back on stream.

By now, at Hodge Close, the Buttermere Company was only working a few small parts of the quarry. Although the quality of the slate had not deteriorated as the quarry went deeper, their main problem was safety. The width of the pit was very narrow at its lowest depths and the Company were very aware of the dangers of working so deep. Any rock falls from the sides would inevitably end up on the narrow quarry floor so work at the base of the pit was eventually abandoned. The main area still being worked was a level known as Back Way which ran in from the south end of the pit. It was accessed by a series of ladders from the top. A few quarrymen were also engaged in working a level in the woods, Bakerstone Barrow Level. Rid from this quarry was trammed across the road to the tip on the other side. Slate from Bakerstone Barrow was of a darker green colour and poor for riving but the Company found some use for it in architectural work. Unfortunately this development was not to save them and eventually in 1964 the whole Hodge Close complex closed down. Although two new private ventures were to start at Tilberthwaite during the 1950s, concern was beginning to grow in the village that hard times were approaching. The closure was just one of a number of incidents that created anxiety. Another was the future of the Coniston Railway.

On the evening of 4th October 1958 the 8.35pm train from Foxfield to Coniston was running almost completely full. This was unusual, this late train was normally virtually empty. But on that particular journey large numbers of passengers embarked at Foxfield and at the intermediate stations. At the various bridges and level crossings along the route small groups of people stood watching the train pass.

On the last leg of the journey from Torver driver Tom Watson sounded the whistle continuously in acknowledgment. Finally, at 9.20pm the train pulled slowly into a crowded Coniston station. Driver Watson and fireman Ron Gaitskell handed it over to a relief crew who drove it back down the branch to Barrow, for the last time. The closure of the passenger service to Coniston was an occasion of great nostalgia and loss to the community. Passenger trains had run for ninety nine years. Goods trains continued to operate, but only until 1962. Complete closure occurred on April 30th of that year.

After closure of the Coniston line all goods had to use road transport. While the goods trains operated, Mandalls continued to use the service, although for a number of years they had made some use of road transport. But the total quantities dispatched were beginning to decline. It was quite clear that, after at least 300 years of operation, the Old Man Quarries were also approaching the end of their life. Mandalls were also beginning to experience financial difficulties and eventually the Company changed hands. A year later, in 1960, the Old Man complex closed completely. The railway had closed and now the quarries were closing as well. These were extremely worrying times for the village. But what nobody knew, at that time, was that the big post-war expansion in Coniston's slate industry was yet to come.

In 1959 an event occurred which was to have a very significant effect on the future of the community. The Lakeland Green Slate and Stone Company decided to re-open the tiny working of Brossen Stone on the east flank of the Old Man. It is difficult to imagine how different Coniston would be today if this event had not occurred. The exploits of this company and the full story of Brossen Stone are described in the next chapter.

THE LAKELAND GREEN SLATE AND STONE Co.

In the years immediately after the Second World War the rural industries in the Lakeland communities slowly returned to normal. Those who were fortunate enough to survive the conflict were thankful when they found that their jobs were still open. For some, however, the experience of the war, and the break from their normal employment, had opened up new horizons and ideas. Many wanted to branch out on their own, perhaps to travel to foreign parts or to start their own ventures.

During the early months of 1948 three Coniston quarrymen decided to form a partnership. They were all keen to re-establish themselves and their intention was to strike out alone to form their own company to quarry slate. The plan was to open a quarry and attempt to make a living by working the stone themselves. But during those early spring months none of them could have anticipated how the venture would go. It is very unlikely that they had any notion of the multi-million pound company that they would ultimately create.

One of the three, Roland Myers, had an idea of where there might be a good 'prospect'. After discussions one night at the Coniston Hunt Ball the three decided to take a look. There were a number of important criteria that must be met and so, the following day, Roland, who lived at Tilberthwaite, took his two colleagues to a place called Moss Rigg in the Tilberthwaite Valley. Here, twenty years previously, the Buttermere Green Slate Company had worked a band of olive green slate. The dip of the slate bed had been very steep and working it had created a deep open pit in the woods at the side of the valley. When Roland and his mates inspected the site they found that the access tunnel into the pit was open and still had the rail lines in place and there was a lot of material that had been discarded on the waste tip which could be re-used. But what caught their eye most was a large clog of slate lying in the base of the pit. It must have been the very last piece of slate block removed from the face by the old Buttermere Company just before the quarry had closed all those years before. It had never made the sawing sheds and had remained there ever since. They estimated that that stone alone could pay their wages for at least two months.

They decided to take the plunge. Roland Myers and his colleagues, George Brownlee from Coniston village and Harold Turnbull from Ridding Head, handed in their notice at their places of work and obtained permission from the National Trust to start working Moss Rigg. The previous owners of the quarry had considered that Moss Rigg slate was unsuitable for riving into roofing slates. But that was twenty years previously. Markets were changing and there was a growing demand for architectural slate as well as a steady requirement for headstones. So

Slate Quarries that have closed over the last 35 years

	Name	**Location**	**Proprietors**
1	Gold Scope	Torver	Gordon Kendal
2	Cove Quarry	Coniston Old Man	Alf Stables
3	Ash Ghyll	Torver	Casson Brockbank
4	Blue Quarry	Coniston Old Man	Mandall's Slate Co Ltd
5	Brandy Crag	"	"
6	Saddlestone	"	"
7	Low Bank	"	"
8	Moss Head	"	"
9	Spion Cop	"	"
10	Penny Rigg	Tilberthwaite	J W Shaw
11	Hodge Close	"	Westmorland Green Slate Co Ltd
12	Parrock	"	"
13	Peat Field	"	"
14	Klondyke	"	"
15	Couter	Great Langdale	Thos Coward & J Rigg
16	Thrang Cragg	"	Thos Coward
17	Banks	"	S Bowness
18	Ewe Crags	Honister	Buttermere Green Slate Co Ltd
19	Hall Garth	Little Langdale	Thos Shaw
20	Common Wood	Ulpha	S Wilson & Partners
21	Owlet Nest	Great Langdale	Pattinsons, Windermere
22	Cawdale Moor	Kirkstone Pass	Thos Shaw & Sons

Slate Quarries re-opened during the last 35 years and still working

1	Brathay	Ambleside	Broughton Moor Green Slate Co
2	Bursting Stone	Coniston Old Man	Mandall's Slate Co Ltd
3	Kirkstone	Ambleside	Kirkstone Green Slate Co Ltd
4	High Fell	Tilberthwaite	J Walker & J Myers
5	Moss Rigg	"	Lakeland Green Slate Co Ltd
6	Spout Crag	Great Langdale	Broughton Moor Green Slate Co

Slate Quarries continually worked for more than the past 35 years

1	Broughton Moor	Torver	Broughton Moor Green Slate Co
2	Elterwater	Great Langdale	"
3	Honister	Buttermere	Buttermere Green Slate Co Ltd

Copy of a document produced in 1965 by George Brownlee of Coniston

the Lakeland Green Slate and Stone Company was established, the lease was obtained from the Buttermere Company and work commenced. The initial idea was to extract walling stone and anything else that was considered useful from the tips. This was sent away by Bill Fury's wagon to Ulverston for sawing. Subsequently, planning permission was obtained to take a twenty foot strip from right round the quarry. There was considerable interest generated in Coniston village when the news of the group's activities became known. Most of the comment seemed to be that they would "get nowt out of yon girt hole."

In the subsequent year the partnership was extended to include Fred Coward. He was an engineer who lived at Holme Ground. It was felt that Fred's background would be invaluable to the new Company. The early days are well remembered by Peggy Myers, wife of Roland. The postman delivered the post to her house in Tilberthwaite and she would go up to Moss Rigg and park her bicycle outside the entrance to the access level. She would then feel her way through the 180 yard tunnel "by putting my foot on the edge of the rails as it was black dark", and hand the post over to her husband. In 1954 another means of access to the working faces was established. A road was constructed that ran up one face of the pit and through a specially constructed cutting at the north east end. The road then ran down through old spoil banks to the processing sheds. The new road allowed much larger clogs of slate to be brought from the quarry to the sheds.

The lack of any sawing facilities was a serious problem. At that time, Mandalls Slate Company were working the Old Man Quarries. They were getting their power from the old turbine in the Coniston Coppermines Valley. This supplied air to the quarries via a three inch diameter pipe which ran up the fellside from the valley to the various banks on the Old Man. Mandalls came to an arrangement with the Lakeland Green Slate and Stone Company that slate clog could be brought up to the Coppermines for sawing at night. An old saw which had once been used to cut blocks from the Blue Quarries was still at the Coppermines and it was brought back into service, taking power from the Mandalls compressed air line. This resulted in a very peculiar working day. The day would start at 7am and work at Moss Rigg would continue until about 3pm. Those who were planning to run the evening shift would go home for a short time and then proceed up to the Coppermines. As soon as the Mandalls Company had finished with the air, sawing would start and would often continue beyond 10pm. Peggy Myers remembers these days well. Occasionally, on a summer evening, she and Roland would walk over the fell from Tilberthwaite to the Coppermines so that Roland could show her a particularly fine piece of slate that had been brought up from Moss Rigg.

It wasn't practical to use this system for very long. The Lakeland Company was expanding and it was decided to move the saw over to Moss Rigg itself. A shed was built on the bank at Moss Rigg, much of the material coming from the old building at the Coppermines. This was a much more practical

Within the sheds in the Coppermines Valley a quarryman rives slate in about 1955. The slate block in the photograph had been quarried from Moss Rigg Quarry in Tilberthwaite, which had been re-opened in 1948 by a group of quarrymen from Coniston.

Within a few months of this photograph being taken the processing operation was moved from the Coppermines Valley to the Moss Rigg Quarry site itself. The shed in which this photograph was taken was dismantled and re-erected at Moss Rigg. Photo – Mike Brownlee

arrangement than previously and the Company now had the basis for steady expansion. Slate block taken from the face in the quarry would be brought through the tunnel along the rail track and out to the processing sheds on the bank. The only material taken away from the site would be finished product. About this time Lakeland also started to attract a high calibre of employee. Highly skilled men such as Ted Coward and Jim Birkett came onto the payroll, which was a good indication of the future potential of the new company. They were two of the most skilled rivers in Coniston.

As the decade progressed so Lakeland Green Slate and Stone Company became established. By 1957 there were 11 men employed. These included Jack Creighton and Billy Blackley who worked the saw and Albert Coward and Geoff Myers who finished the riven slates. A "Jenny Lind" polishing machine was installed which was operated by Albert Pepper and was used to give a mirror-like finish to slate blocks. The Company successfully negotiated some important contracts including the British Engine Insurance Building in the centre of Manchester. This job was worth over £40,000 and put the Company on their feet. At that time it was the largest green slate cladding contract ever awarded.

Another major contract which was successfully completed in the early 1960s was to provide over 25,000 square feet of naturally riven slate for the new Coventry Cathedral. Both the Chapel of Unity and the Guild Chapel were furnished with Moss Rigg slate and a number of the employees attended the opening ceremony in 1962.

It was very obvious to the directors of the Company that there was a demand for light green slate. Moss Rigg produced an olive green product. The market leaders at that time, Broughton Moor Ltd. had been promoting their lighter slates which they were obtaining at Elterwater, Spout Crag and, to a certain extent, Broughton Moor. It was felt that it was essential that the Lakeland Company obtained a source of lighter green material. But the question on everybody's minds was how they should go about it.

High above Coniston village, on the slopes of Coniston Old Man, the Mandalls Company worked the Old Man Quarries. The highest of these workings were at an altitude of over 2000ft. During the 1950s Mandalls started to experience financial difficulties and in 1959 Lakeland took them over. This was a very bold move for Lakeland because Mandalls, although declining in recent years, was still a much bigger company. The main jewel in Mandall's crown, however, was not the Old Man Quarries, which many felt were largely approaching the end of their life, but a small and ancient quarry on the south east face of the mountain. Over a hundred years earlier Brossen Stone had been worked for a short while by the 'old men'. After only a few years of activity it had closed. It was generally felt that there may still be good deposits of light green slate at Brossen Stone and the Lakeland Company decided that it should be re-opened.

As rock working techniques improved larger and larger blocks of slate could be brought from the face with much less wastage. In this photograph, taken in the 1970s at Brossen Stone on Coniston Old Man, the quarry foreman, George Coward oversees the working of one large block of slate, part of which was destined to became the memorial to Lord Mountbatten.

Photo provided by A Walker, source unknown

Brossen Stone was the key to considerable expansion for the Lakeland Company. During the summer months a road was constructed up the flank of the mountain. The site of the old workings was cleared. The tiny level was opened out and, within a very short space of time, good deposits of two shades of light green slate were confirmed. This was the key to considerable progress. The Company soon built up to a work force in excess of sixty men and started competing successfully with their old rivals, Broughton Moor, for sizable contracts. Clearly, potential customers considered the new company was competent to supply to the required quality, and their costings and lead-times were favourable.

Had it not been for the opening of Brossen, there would have been little competition within the market, and it is unlikely that the Lake District green slate industry would have operated so successfully over the next thirty years. As it was, a considerable export industry started to develop with both companies competing for many world wide contracts. Modern sales and marketing techniques were also developed by both Lakeland and Broughton Moor with each trying to steal an edge on the other. This competition resulted in a very high level of promotion of architectural slate world-wide. Both the German and US markets opened up, followed soon after by the Middle and Far East. By now many of the most prestigious buildings in the world were being clad with slate from either Brossen Stone or one of the Broughton Moor quarries.

Perhaps we should dwell for a few minutes on the fact that, if the 'environmentalists' of the day had had their way, and Brossen Stone had not been developed, the livelihood of the South Lakeland communities based on Coniston would have suffered severely and a whole, valuable, export industry would not have developed.

Because Brossen was becoming so successful it was decided to halt production at Moss Rigg. For a second time in its existence the Company had to consider its processing facilities. Moss Rigg was some distance away from the site of extraction and eventually a new processing building was constructed at Brossen Stone itself. However this was not before a costly planning appeal by Lakeland against a decision by the Lake District Special Planning Board.

The Planning Board had turned down the plans by the Company for a processing plant at Coniston Copper Mines. The appeal was heard at a public inquiry held in Coniston village. Understandably there was considerable support by local people for Lakeland's plans. Coniston Copper Mines was not far from Brossen Stone. It would avoid the six mile journey from there to Moss Rigg. A short road would be constructed round the flank of Coniston Old Man from Brossen to the proposed site. The Coniston Parish Council voiced their support. So did Bill Shaw, from Coniston's well-known mining family and also Jim Cameron, the distinguished Lakeland mountaineer. But the voice of the environmentalist was to carry the day. Most of those against the plans did not originate from Coniston.

They included Geoffrey Berry, secretary of the 'Friends of the Lake District', Eric Holland, who had written about the Coppermines, the YHA, who ran a hostel at the mines and The Fell and Rock Climbing Club. It had been an expensive operation and had focused quite sharply on the rift between the environmental 'off-comer' and the local community.

In 1962 Mike Brownlee, son of George, one of the founders, came to the Company. Mike had been working for the civil engineering firm, Laings and was, eventually, to take over the running of the Lakeland Company.

During the late '60s Lord Richard Cavendish, chairman of Burlington Slate at Kirkby in Furness, struck up a personal friendship with George Brownlee. Lord Cavendish was very keen to take an interest in a green slate quarry. He had plenty of blue-grey slate down at Kirkby. But the market required light green slate and, at Brossen Stone, Lakeland now had probably the best source of light green slate in the country. Fred Coward had, by this time, died. Roland Myers and Harold Turnbull both decided to sell their interest in the Company and this was taken up by Lord Cavendish. George Brownlee retained his share holding and an agreement was reached between the Brownlee family and Lord Cavendish that the Brownlees would continue to run Lakeland. This state of affairs continued until Richard Cavendish died in 1972.

In general, there was a feeling in the industry that there was already too much competition. Both Broughton Moor and Lakeland frequently found themselves competing for contracts from around the world. Some joint projects did take place, an example being in 1973 when both companies were jointly awarded a contract to supply slate for cladding the new city centre complex of Mainz in Germany. At the time it was the biggest green-slate contract ever awarded. But in general the Broughton Moor Company felt that both Lakeland and Kirkstone were a threat and should be taken over. Over the next few years the industry did retract, but not as the Broughton Moor Company had anticipated.

It was the objective of the Cavendish family to own all the South Cumbria slate concerns. In 1975 Broughton Moor was taken over by Lord Cavendish's Burlington Company. Some years before, the previous owners, the Cann family, had sold the concern to The Delabole Company of Cornwall. This was to offset death duties that the family had incurred. For the employees of Broughton Moor, the period under Delabole was uncertain to say the least and news of the take-over was greeted with relief. This resulted in a situation where Burlington owned the whole of the Kirkby complex and the quarries of Broughton Moor, Elterwater, Spout Crag and Brathay and a majority portion of Lakeland Green Slate and Stone and also Mandalls. This was very close to being a monopoly situation.

In 1975 George Brownlee died. His son, Mike, continued running Lakeland until, in 1979, he sold out his share to the Cavendish family. All the manufacturing and marketing resources of the Lakeland Company became integrated into Burlington Slate. Lord Cavendish now controlled the whole of the South Lakeland slate industry, with the exception of a few small operators. Under his control, the industry experienced many years of prosperity. Despite the closing of Spout Crag and Brathay quarries, slate quarrying has continued as a viable industry in the village right up to recent times.

Photo provided by Mrs P Tromans

NEW BEGINNINGS

During the middle years of the 20th Century the economic climate in Britain was not conducive to the small operator. The economy of scale was beginning to be the dominant consideration. Big was beautiful and the smaller rural industries started to close down More recently the pendulum has begun to swing the other way. Within the slate industry in Lakeland small companies which are flexible and are prepared to take on modest, diverse orders are beginning to find a niche. The planning authorities are also much more relaxed about smaller operations which are wholly within their concept of a working National Park and which are keeping alive a traditional industry with a history going back nearly 1000 years.

A great many Lakeland quarries closed down prior to the Second World War, not because slate reserves became exhausted but because they were uneconomic to operate within the existing economic culture.

Since the war several quarries have re-opened and the exploits of those who have been instrumental in this are described below.

High Fell Greenslate Co. Ltd.

Jim Walker left Coniston school in 1944 at the age of 13. For the next three years he worked on a number of local farms. It was his father who advised him to leave farming and become an apprentice river at the Broughton Moor Green Slate Company. After a brief period in the army he returned to Broughton Moor for a further six year spell. It was during this time he started to consider working for himself. He was well aware of the exploits of the Lakeland Company at Moss Rigg and felt that, if he could find a suitable location, he might be able to set up in a similar way. So in 1957, with two colleagues, Frank Shaw and Geoff Myers, he negotiated a ten-year lease with the National Trust for High Fell Quarry and started work.

High Fell is situated at an altitude of 1100ft above the Tilberthwaite Valley and about three miles north of Coniston. Access is by a steep rough cart road from the valley. The quarry had not been worked for at least twenty years since the Buttermere Green Slate Company ceased all their operations in the Coniston area. Most of the quarrying that had been carried out by the old company had been underground and Jim and his colleagues started by clearing the closehead ready to resume extraction. In 1959 the group were joined by Jim Myers, father of Geoff. For a brief period in the early 1960s the new company joined forces with another concern in Kendal. Within a few years the two businesses split again, High Fell being operated by Jim Walker and Jim Myers. In 1972 Neville Walker, Jim's son, joined them. In 1975 Jim Myers retired, aged 67 years.

For many years now the old closehead has been abandoned and all the slate is obtained from small open-top quarries close by. Most of the product from High Fell now consists of slabs and tiles. A workshop has been built on the main bank which is capable of processing slate completely from rough blocks brought out of the quarry into finished finely polished product. The father and son team were proud that they controlled the complete operation from working the face, transporting the stone to the workshop, sawing and polishing, delivering to the customer and, when time permitted, doing a bit of selling as well.

More recently Jim Walker has retired and George Tarr has joined Neville to work the quarry.

Horse Crag

Another example of entrepreneurial flair relates to the re-opening of Horse Crag Quarry by George Tarr. George has been associated with the slate industry all his life. In 1969 he started work at Brossen Stone Quarry on Coniston Old Man at the age of 17. He served his time there as a rockhand. More recently he has been employed by a local builder in Coniston. However while in the quarries George has worked at Spout Crag and also Brathay Quarry as well as Brossen Stone.

In 1989 he began to think about starting up on his own. Slate quarrying was in his blood and, rather than return to working for Burlington Slate, he wanted to see if he could make a go of his own venture. He started to look around for a suitable location. The main criteria in choosing a site were three-fold: accessibility, potential for good quality slate and also a location which would be approved by the Lake District National Park Authority.

Choosing the best location was not easy. There were many disused workings which had fine deposits of slate but which were completely inaccessible. Others were far too open and would never have the approval of the planning authorities. In the end George chose Horse Crag underground working in Tilberthwaite.

Horse Crag has had an interesting history which has been described in the earlier chapter 'Between the Wars'. It had been worked for a period of about eight years in the 1930s by Coniston miner John Willie Shaw. He had worked a pocket of slate that had been discovered (but not exploited) by copper miners driving a level nearly a hundred years earlier. Shaw had abandoned the venture in August 1938 because he felt he was too old to continue. His efforts had resulted in a sizable closehead about 300ft along the old level.

George Tarr felt that there was potential at Horse Crag. In 1989 he applied to the planning authorities to start working the underground chamber. Eventually this was granted with some provisions including the requirement not to dispose of any waste rock outside. It all had to remain in the closehead.

High above the quarry floor George Tarr drills shot holes at the High Fell Quarry.
Photo – George Tarr

He planned to work the quarry in the evenings and at weekends. When he first started he spent all his spare time there. He first cleared the level and reinstated the rail track. He then installed lighting and compressed air and he has even constructed his own wire saw unit. One of his sons and several of his friends have been very keen to lend a hand. The previous tenant had robbed the closehead badly and George found it necessary to put in a lot of work before the working faces could be re-established. At the present time the quarry has been mothballed as George has other commitments elsewhere.

It is fairly certain that Horse Crag is one of two last working slate mines in England and George has received a lot of interest and encouragement from a large number of people during the project. The planning authorities have also been keen to watch developments. To them this is just the type of venture that they want to see being set up in the Lake District.

Hodge Close

In 1987 Sam Dugdale obtained the lease to work the Peat Field site at Hodge Close from the Egremont Estates. Sam had worked in the slate industry since leaving school twenty years previously. During his early years of employment he had gained experience at several of the large South Lakeland quarries but his ambition had always been to manage his own operation.

Peat Field quarry, in the woods below Holme Ground cottages, had been worked by the Tilberthwaite Green Slate Company until the company's demise after the First World War. Since then little work had been carried out but there was still a considerable quantity of slate present at Peat Field and also in the underground chambers of Klondike Quarry which were more or less directly underneath.

It took Sam some time to negotiate planning permission from the Lake District Special Planning Board. Having obtained permission he started to acquire the necessary equipment. Two other men joined him and for the next seven years the operation expanded steadily. Since 1987 the new Company has built up an impressive quantity of equipment including a slate saw and heavy vehicles. Most of the product is roofing slate although a full range of slate products including flooring tiles can be produced. The Company carry out all the work themselves from working the face within the quarry to completing the product ready for delivery. Much of the quarry rid is disposed of into the nearby Hodge Close pit.

Some years after Peat Field was re-opened Sam turned his attention to the abandoned Brathay Quarry. This quarry, in the woods near Skelwith, had been worked on and off for nearly 200 years. Brathay slate was very unusual and of an extremely high quality. It had been worked by the Broughton Moor Company as a slab quarry for nine years (see 'The Cann Story') until they closed it in 1975, convinced that there was no more workable slate present. Sam was sure that this was not the case. He hired a pump and started to pump out the old workings. Within a short space of time he had obtained good quality slate. But as well as material for slabs he had also found excellent riving slate. One of Sam's most prestigious orders was for sixty tons of roofing slate for White Cross Bay leisure complex at Windermere which he produced entirely from stone from Brathay.

The 1990s were very difficult years for Sam, not the least because of the cost of maintaining expensive plant and machinery which was essential for his work. He eventually sold the operation to two other very competent Coniston quarrymen, Billy Gibson and Martin Askew. Under these new operators the workings developed further. Billy and Martin eventually sold the lease for Peat Field to Burlington Slate.

Quarry smith

RECENT TIMES

This book is intended primarily to be a history of the Coniston slate industry and it is not proposed to go into great detail about the present day operation. However the history would not be complete without considering briefly the important events that have happened over the past fifty years which have affected the industry and the village community in general.

Within five years of the Bursting Stone Quarry coming on stream, it had started to make a considerable contribution to the local economy as well as to the fortunes of the Lakeland Green Slate Company. Effectively this marked the start of a new era for Coniston and its slate industry.

At the same time, the village was seeing significant changes taking place as a result of tourism and improved road access to the Lake District. The pressure of tourism started to increase considerably. This was not just felt by an increase in the number of visitors, which the village was quite capable of absorbing, but also by the desire of many to acquire 'second homes' in the village, which effectively removed from the market just the type of accommodation that working families required. A survey carried out in the early 1970s showed a very high proportion of property, in fact as much as 20%, was in this category. Quite a proportion of second home owners planned to move to the village on retirement, but those who did frequently found that it was not ideal for them. Their roots were not in the village and eventually they would move back to their area of origin.

Other pressures started to bear on the local community and its livelihood. These came from 'environmental' groups who began to become concerned about the effect of the slate industry on visual aspects of the Lake District. One organisation, 'The Friends of the Lake District', became very active during the 1970s and, to local people, seemed intent on closing down the slate industry in its entirety. A number of long and heated battles followed at public inquiries and in the press. To the community, many of these environmentalists were seen as 'off-comers' who, having already removed a proportion of the local cottages from the housing market, were now intent on closing down the very industry on which the community had relied for centuries.

In reality there were probably faults on both sides. Modern quarrying techniques bear little comparison to the traditional slate industry pre-1960, and the quarry owners displayed an unfortunate indifference to environmental issues. On the other hand many of those who had moved to the village totally failed to understand the culture of the community and appreciate the need for a rural industry other than tourism. Fortunately these disputes are now a thing of the past. The slate industry is now accepted by most as an essential part of the local life.

The Moss Head Closehead within Coniston Old Man was developed during the 20th Century and, when the Old Man Quarries closed in 1959, had become a sizeable complex of chambers.

Photo – A Cameron

The Lake District National Park authority is very aware of this and has stated, in its Structure Plan Policy, that, *"The continued working of slate quarries as a traditional industry is accepted. Proposals for new quarries and extensions to existing quarries will be assessed in accordance with the criteria set out in Policy 10-1A with particular regard to the effect on the landscape and the local community."*

The area's largest landowner, The National Trust, has also mellowed in recent times and appreciates the careful balance that is required. But the 'track record' of the National Trust is certainly not perfect. In 1973 it closed down the small and unobtrusive Dalt green slate quarry in Borrowdale because of its potential impact on the environment, despite the fact that it supported ten local families. However at the time of writing this book the Trust are actively negotiating to re-open the Guards Quarry in Yewdale to provide local flag stone for building work.

There is considerable potential today for other old surface and underground workings to be re-opened and worked in a more traditional way that would not adversely affect the environment. This has already started to happen and it is hoped that further small operations will start up in the future.

One reason why visitors were flocking to Coniston in the late 1950s was to witness the attempts by Donald Campbell in his boat *Bluebird* to raise progressively the world water speed record. On several occasions in the late 1950s he was successful but for a period of about six years he abandoned Coniston for venues in Australia and the United States. In November 1966 he returned to his base at the Sun Hotel in Coniston.

While having his breakfast on the morning of January 4th 1967, quarryman Tommy Gregg became aware that Campbell was about to have another attempt on the record. Conditions were perfect and Tommy decided not to catch the quarry wagon to work at Broughton Moor but to go down to the shore on the east side of the lake and watch the attempt from there. He saw *Bluebird*'s first run down the lake and then waited for the return. He watched the blue craft skim up the lake – and then somersault and disappear below the surface. Tommy drove up to Broughton Moor to break the news to his workmates. Campbell's death had a most profound effect on the village, even today most Coniston people can remember quite clearly where they were and what they were doing at the time of the accident. A memorial in slate from Broughton Moor was constructed in the village, the lettering of which Tommy had the honour to engrave.

With Bursting Stone becoming established the two major slate companies operating in Coniston set up modern offices in the village from which their manufacturing and sales operations could be administered. The Lakeland Company converted a house at Yewdale Bridge into offices. Broughton Moor built a prestigious showroom at its offices at Wraysdale House on the Torver road, a few

A familiar sight today on the fells above Coniston are the yellow trucks which carry the large clogs of slate down the valley to Kirkby in Furness for processing. Two skilled Coniston drivers, Dickie Walker and John Robinson, have been responsible for this part of Burlington's operations for many years. In this photograph Dickie is driving his truck above the Coppermines Valley to collect slate from the Low Brandy Crag workings.

Photo – A Cameron

hundred yards from the village centre. From these two headquarters the rival companies competed for slate contracts right across the world. It must have been quite a surprise to the architects of the spectacular Bank of California building in Portland, Oregon when they received two rival bids for slate cladding from the same small village in Northern England.

In 1970, when Burlington Slate took over the Broughton Moor Company, the Coniston offices were retained. Nine years later Burlington also took over the Lakeland Company as well and, for a period of time, offices were moved to Brigg House, Torver, before returning to Coniston into a brand new headquarters, Cavendish House, which had been built on the site of the old Broughton Moor offices.

As the industry entered the 1980s the outlook appeared healthy. The new Burlington Company operated quarries at Kirkby Moor in Low Furness, Broughton Moor, Moss Rigg and Brossen Stone and, in Langdale, at Elterwater and Spout Crag. Processing facilities were retained at most sites allowing the manufacture of slate products to be carried on at the quarries. The product portfolio was extensive with most of the natural slate colours represented. However there was one type of slate that was not being worked.

For hundreds of years Coniston's silver-grey slate had been quarried on the Old Man. It had produced the best riving slate in Lakeland. But the old Mandall Company, who operated the Old Man Quarries, had run 'out of steam'. When Lakeland had taken them over in 1960 the demand was for slate with a green tinge and the Lakeland Company had put all their efforts into establishing Brossen Stone on the light green slate band. Now, twenty five years later, it was felt that there could again be a demand for slate from the silver-grey band.

During August 1982 work began to construct a bridge over Levers Water Beck in the Coppermines Valley. Within a fortnight the bridge was complete and contractors, using heavy earth-moving machinery, had started to build a road across the marshy depression known as Levers Moss towards the lowest slopes of Coniston Old Man. Here, several centuries ago, the 'old men' had worked a tiny underground quarry on the silver-grey band which they named Low Brandy Crag. A level had been driven by hand and a small closehead had been opened out. But they had failed to find the extensive deposits of slate that did, in fact, exist there. The work had been abandoned.

With the completion of the road, heavy equipment could be brought right up to Low Brandy Crag. A pneumatic well-boring rig and a face shovel started to open out the old working. The extensive deposits of slate were soon located. Before long the old workings had been cleared completely and a quarry face established. Silver-grey slate was once more being extracted from the Coniston Fells.

Slate clog from Low Brandy Crag Quarry was taken away for processing elsewhere. Eventually all slate from the Coniston quarries would be taken by heavy truck down to the Company's site at Kirkby for processing. This was outside the confines of the Lake District National Park. In 1987 the Coniston offices were closed and all administration was also transferred to larger premises at Kirkby. Those living in Coniston who worked for the Company now had to make the daily journey down to Kirkby. In 1995 Burlington Slate announced that they were planning to open a slate museum at the Kirkby site. This was welcome news. The project would quite clearly become a major tourist attraction but there were those who felt that Coniston would have made a much more fitting venue for such an enterprise. Due to planning difficulties the project at Kirkby was eventually abandoned.

Today Burlington Slate operate internationally from offices in London, the United States and their head office at Kirkby. The Company have been at the forefront of development in the industry in recent years. They have experimented with mechanical riving and dressing machines and also with improved ways of working the faces at the quarries. Since 1988 wire saws have been in use at all their quarries to cut rock, saving considerably on wastage. There is also a significant market developing in crushed stone for decorative use in gardens and other outdoor areas. This has been pioneered by Donald Kelly, manager of their Elterwater site. In 2003 the Company acquired the private Peat Field operation at Hodge Close. Both the former owners of the Peat Field quarry came onto the Company's pay roll.

The history of slate from Coniston has now reached the present day. But the contrast between the present and the past is quite remarkable. Only sixty years ago quarrymen sat in their riving sheds at Hodge Close manufacturing roofing slate by hand. Today they work in purpose built workshops. Then they provided slate to roof terraced houses in northern cities. Today they provide slate for decorative features and external cladding of prestigious buildings round the world.

Viewing the slate market today it is quite clear that two separate industries exist with very different markets. In Seattle the residence of Bill Gates, president of the Microsoft Corporation features greenslate from Elterwater for much of its structure. This has been manufactured by Burlington using the latest laser-guided equipment. Meanwhile, high above Tilberthwaite, on the lower slopes of Wetherlam, Neville Walker and George Tarr work slate from their quarry to produce tiles of the highest quality. Their saws are guided by the human eye (and a skilled hand) and their customers are scattered round the North of England. The future of slate from Coniston lies as much in their hands as in the hands of those who operate the laser-guided saws.

As time goes on the visual remains of former slate workings mellow into the surroundings. Fifty years ago these tips of the Calf Howe workings in Tilberthwaite would have been very prominent to anyone walking from High Tilberthwaite to Little Langdale. Over the intervening period trees have grown up and moss covers the older tips. Today it is very easy to walk past the Calf Howe workings without even noticing them.

THE FORMATION OF SLATE

What exactly is slate? How has it been formed and why is it possible to split or 'rive' it into thin, flat, durable sheets? It is certainly a strange phenomenon that allows a lump of rock to be split so evenly and exactly, into such thin sections with such perfection.

How can one define 'slate'? How best can we describe this unusual material? Defining it accurately is not easy and probably the best definition that can be applied is the simple one proposed by McFadzean which is that slate is 'a fine grained rock that possesses the ability to cleave evenly and uniformly. If it does not cleave, then it is not slate!!'. The term 'slate' is frequently used incorrectly. Geologists of old described the ancient rocks of the northern Lakes as Skiddaw Slates. Technically these rocks are not slate at all. They will not cleave and their name is inaccurate.

'Slate' is not one particular type of stone. It can vary considerably in chemical constituency, geological age, method of formation, colour, texture and general physical characteristics. But as long as it can be cleaved, then, by our definition, it is 'slate'.

Rock which conforms to our definition can be found in most continents of the world and from many geological periods. Belgium, France, Spain, North Africa, North and South America are just a few locations where cleavable slate has been extracted commercially. In the UK the best quality slates originate from a number of geological periods as shown on the map on the following page.

The 'youngest' slate worked in the UK is from the massive Delabole workings in Cornwall and was deposited during the Devonian Period, approximately 350 million years ago. The colour varies from greenish-grey to dark blue.

Cumbrian slates are either Silurian (approximately 410 million years old) or Ordovician (460 million years old). The Ffestiniog and Corris slates of Wales are also Ordovician but those from the Bethesda–Nantlle belt are from the Cambrian era and therefore older at about 500 million years. Welsh slates tend to be very dark and of uniform texture. They cleave well but lack the pleasing green shade and striking markings that make the volcanic slate from Cumbria so attractive.

The oldest slates extracted in the UK are from the once extensive Scottish workings. They represent the Pre-Cambrian period and are more than 600 million years old. Scottish slate is very dark, almost black in colour, but contains impurities which will weather out when exposed. This tends to result in open voids

103

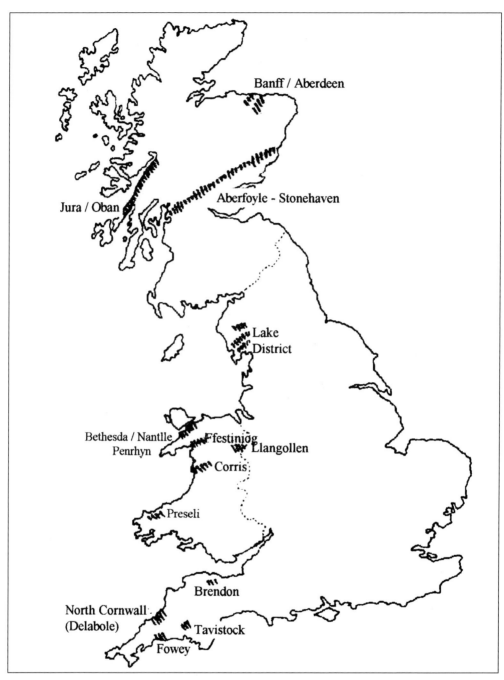

The major slate production areas in the United Kingdom

forming in finished slates after a number of years on the roof of a building. By the 1950s all slate extraction in Scotland ceased.

Geologists have argued over the centuries as to how slate beds were formed. At the present time there seems to be general agreement amongst them as to how this has occurred. There are two different types of slate deposits at Coniston which have been laid down in two totally separate ways. These are volcanic slates and sedimentary slates. This makes it even more difficult for the lay-person to grasp the technical details, and some knowledge of the geology of the Coniston area is necessary before it becomes clear.

It is presently believed that in the middle of the Ordovician Age volcanic activity caused the rocks of the central Lakeland area to form. This activity continued on and off for over one million years, discharging lavas and ashes to a height which is estimated to have been up to 15,000ft. Much of the material that was thrown out has long since been swept away by more recent events but enough still remains to cover an area of some 400 square miles. It is generally referred to as the Borrowdale Volcanic Group and covers much of Central Lakeland.

Coniston village lies right at the edge of this great mass of volcanic rock. To the north and west of the village the mountains are part of the Volcanic Group. To the south and east of the village the low rolling hills are not volcanic. They are of totally different rock of sedimentary origin caused by material settling out of flowing streams. These hills stretch away to the coast. Sedimentary rock is not the result of volcanic activity. Between the two types of rock is a narrow band of limestone known as the Coniston Limestone which is, in places, only a few hundred meters wide. The limestone is first seen near Millom and runs across Torver High Common, through the Yewdale Valley and then away towards Shap passing the head of Windermere Lake.

To the north west, in the Lakeland mountains, the beds of the Borrowdale Volcanic Series exist as many types and textures of rock. Part of the beds consist of slate 'bands'. These were not formed from the volcanic lavas and agglomerates, but from fine volcanic ash and dust which fell to the ground at the same time and settled in shallow lakes. There are three beds of slate within the rocks at the base of the Volcanic Series and the slate here has been worked in the Honister area. Near the top of the Volcanic series are seven or eight beds and three of these have been worked extensively in southern Lakeland, especially at Coniston. Between the top and base beds, the volcanic heart of Lakeland is virtually completely devoid of slate.

But volcanic activity was only the start of the process to form slate. Further changes were yet to come. Slate rock is referred to as a metamorphosed rock, in other words, it has been greatly altered some time after it was originally deposited and it is this alteration that has created the unique properties of slate.

105

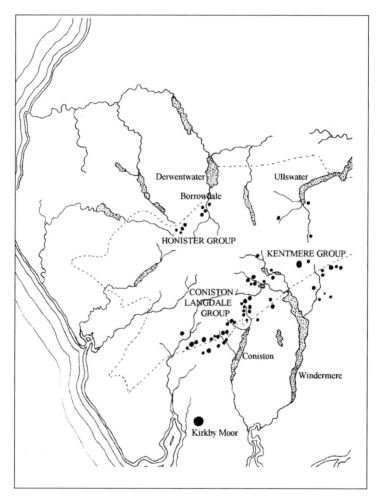

Locations of the majority of slate mines and quarries in Cumbria. Also shown by the dashed line is the extent of the Borrowdale Volcanic Group, the volcanic heartland of Lakeland. The workings outside the area were mainly within sedimentary beds of slate. At Coniston these workings produced predominantly slabs and flags.

The alteration to the beds was caused, it is thought, by tremendous pressures and increased temperatures that the land masses were subjected to when the continents collided. This occurred during the onset of the Devonian period and resulted in a folding of the earth's surface.

The continental collision affected the slate rock in two ways. Firstly it caused the microscopic silicate particles of material making up the beds of ash to re-orientate from the original horizontal axis or 'bedding plane' on which they had been laid down to a near vertical axis. In some rock the re-orientation was very consistent and uniform and as a result the material now had the ability to split very cleanly along the new line or orientation of the particles. The result of this phenomenon is cleavage, or 'bate' as it is known by the quarrymen. This new line of orientation, known as the cleavage plane, often lies at a considerable angle (sometimes 90 deg) to the original 'bedding plane'. This frequently surprises the lay person watching a skilled river at work. The slate appears to be splitting across the bandings in a piece of rock rather than along them.

The second effect was to alter the angle of the slate bed from the original horizontal angle to one which, where the land mass had become extremely folded, could be nearly vertical. At Coniston the strata was steeply folded and the slate beds ultimately came to lie along a north-east/south-west axis.

The beds worked at Coniston did not consist entirely of riveable slate. In places the beds were devoid of good slate 'metal' completely. In some areas such as on Coniston Old Man it was fairly well established but in others it had to be looked for. Where slate outcropped to the surface it would be quite evident to the keen cycs of the 18th and 19th Century quarryman. But where deposits existed sporadically beneath the hillsides, a degree of luck was required. However, finding good deposits was not totally a matter of chance. Some Coniston quarrymen quite clearly had a 'nose' for it when working in an area; an ability which is known locally as 'being able to see through rock'.

The 'old men' knew that slate was hard to find. That is why the earliest quarries were situated high on the rocky outcrops where it was possible, for the experienced eye, to discern the faint, rippling pattern of the bate beneath the moss and lichen. On the Old Man the weathered bate patterns are quite distinctive. The craggy outcrops above Scald Cop consist of good slate that has been subjected to thousands of years of erosion. The weather has penetrated the stone and etched the striated pattern so carefully that it is as if the whole mass has been painstakingly riven by a giant hand where it stands. In no other location can the phenomenon of bate be observed more clearly than on the summit. In this high place, close to the cairn, the passing of time and tramping of boots has revealed the rock, perfectly riven, raking through the heart of the mountain towards distant Walna Scar Quarries.

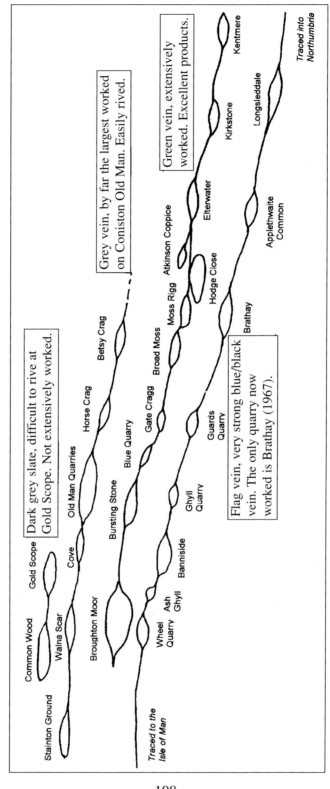

Dark grey slate, difficult to rive at Gold Scope. Not extensively worked.

Grey vein, by far the largest worked on Coniston Old Man. Easily rived.

Green vein, extensively worked. Excellent products.

Flag vein, very strong blue/black vein. The only quarry now worked is Brathay (1967).

Common Wood

Stainton Ground

Gold Scope

Walna Scar

Cove

Old Man Quarries

Broughton Moor

Horse Crag

Betsy Crag

Bursting Stone

Blue Quarry

Gate Cragg

Broad Moss

Moss Rigg

Atkinson Coppice

Elterwater

Kirkstone

Kentmere

Hodge Close

Longsleddale

Traced to the Isle of Man

Wheel Quarry

Ash Ghyll

Banniside

Ghyll Quarry

Guards Quarry

Brathay

Applethwaite Common

Traced into Northumbria

Reproduction of a drawing made by George Brownlee in 1967 depicting the slate bands worked in the South Lakeland area.

The low lying land to the south and east of Coniston consists purely of sedimentary rocks. Surprisingly, some slate has been extracted from these rocks as well, but it is all sedimentary slate rather than volcanic. This slate has been formed by water-borne particles being deposited as large sedimentary beds. These deposits were also subjected to metamorphism in a similar way to the volcanic deposits.

At Kirkby, in Low Furness, massive beds of sedimentary slate were formed and these have been worked for over 300 years giving high quality product with a blue-grey/black colour. At Coniston a narrow bed of sedimentary slate runs through the upper limit of the sedimentary rock close to and parallel with the Coniston Limestone. In the main this bed did not produce the quality roofing slates as did the nearby volcanic rock. Quarries on this band include Brathay, Guards, Coniston Ghyll, Banniside (Tranearth) and Ash Gill. Over the past centuries these quarries have been worked as much for flags and slabs as for roofing slate.

So slate is not one particular type of rock. It is purely rock which has the ability to be riven. Quarrymen are particular about what is slate and what is not. One face of a quarry could be identical to the next, the rock could be the same colour, the same age, possess the same chemical composition but if the bate is not present, it is not slate. Instead it is 'crag'...... 'bastard-rock'..... 'muck'.

The different beds in the Volcanic Series produced different coloured slates because of their varying chemical compositions. The highest bed at Coniston gave a dark blue/green slate but this was not extensively worked. Gold Scope Quarries were situated on this bed and produced slate which was found to be difficult to split. The next bed is the famous 'Silver-grey Band' which was worked extensively on Coniston Old Man, and at Cove and Walna Scar as well as at Horse Crag and Betsy Crag in Tilberthwaite. The lowest of the three bands worked is the 'Green Band'. This was worked at Elterwater, Hodge Close and Moss Rigg, Blue Quarry, Brossen Stone and Broughton Moor. The intensity of the green colour could vary considerably within this bed. At Moss Rigg the slate was a dark olive green while at Brossen Stone the shade varied from dark green to a much lighter green. There was also a considerable difference between the grain and texture of the slate.

The slate bands can be intersected by a number of joints and faults which, although spoiling the slate rock to a certain extent, can assist the rockhands to extract the clogs. The small joints are variously known as heads, seams, wrinkles and rowls. Heads and seams are indistinct fractures in the rock. Rowls and wrinkles are vertical anomalies displacing the bate by an inch or two. The largest and most recognisable joints are called slipes. These generally follow the direction of the bed, are of infinite length and depth and are frequently mineralised mainly with quartz or pyrite. Wherever possible the miners who were employed to drive the levels did so along the edge of the slipes. They were aware that the rock would blast away cleanly and easily. Fewer shot holes were required, less dynamite was used and less good slate 'metal' was damaged unnecessarily.

The methods used by quarrymen to work slate in each locality depended on the nature of the rock and the way it had been formed. The next section will describe how skilled quarrymen worked a face taking account of the rock strata and faults to produce a quality product as economically as possible.

Photo by Ted Bowness

THE EXTRACTION OF SLATE

From the very earliest times until well within living memory slate rock was extracted, riven and dressed under a universal system of payment which was known as the Bargain System. By this system, at regular intervals, which could be as frequent as monthly, a price was agreed between the owners of the quarry and a 'Company' of men for the tonnage of slate that was to be produced from a particular face in a period of time.

There were normally four or five men in a Company and each Company negotiated its own bargain with the owners. A typical Company consisted of two rockhands who worked the face, two rivers and a dresser. The price agreed between the owners and the Company varied according to the quality of rock in the face. If the output that was expected was low, because the rock appeared poor or looked as if it would be difficult to extract, the price agreed would be high. However if the face showed good rock and promised a high yield, a lower price would be agreed. Quite often the dresser was 'shared' between several Companies. The bargain system is one of the best indications the historians have that the skills and practices within the industry came over from mainland Europe with William the Conqueror in the eleventh century. The Company system is virtually identical to that which operated in the slate mining areas of Belgium and France for over a thousand years.

One of the earliest references to the Company system at Coniston is from the 1770s when, at Cove Quarries on the east face of Coniston Old Man, at least two Companies were active. Zachias Walker & Company were working Low Cove while, above, John Massachs & Company were at Middle Cove. On the other side of the mountain, William Atkinson & Company were quarrying at Scald Cop. These groups actually produced the slates and were paid by the slate merchant for the tonnage they turned out. The merchant, in turn, paid royalties to Lady le Fleming, the mineral owner, for the quantity of finished slates that went down the mountain.

There are still retired quarrymen in Coniston who can remember the Company system, the monthly payouts and the 'bargain-setting'. In the Lake District, proprietors were happy to see it survive. Not so in North Wales where, during the 19th Century, efforts were repeatedly made to introduce various restrictive piece works and contracting-out systems. This resulted in lengthy strikes, lock-outs and the infamous riots at Penrhyn, Dinorwic and other Welsh quarries.

The Company system effectively meant that the men were self employed. After the Second World War a number of new operations started and as they

111

'Roundheads'

The action of frost has caused this slate outcrop to split along the 'bate' or 'cleavage plane' which, in this case, is nearly vertical. There is evidence that, in the 18th Century; slate cleaved naturally this way would be collected by the dalesmen and used to provide rough slabs for domestic or farm use. This particular outcrop is at Blake Rigg, on the lower slopes of Wetherlam.

Photo – Peter Fleming

This collection of photographs shows the development in the techniques for working slate over the past centuries in the Lakeland area.

The earliest technique involved prizing slate from surface deposits. We believe that Roman and early Norman extraction would have been by this method. Slate outcropped to the surface at several locations in the Coniston area. Two such outcrops are shown here; near the summit of Coniston Old Man and on Kitty Crag.

113

Subsequently, as extraction from surface deposits continued in a particular location, a cutting would be formed. Several of these early working sites have been identified on the fells above Coniston (above).

Eventually, if slate extraction continued at a particular site, a 'cave-working' developed. These workings could become quite large and there are estimates that some of them were in operation for over three hundred years.

Because of their size and close proximity to the surface the roofs frequently became very unstable. Many collapsed including two large cave workings on the Old Man. The ones shown here have survived.

Cave workings were not favoured by quarry proprietors because of the dangers and difficulties that occurred during operations. After about 1700 all new underground quarry development used techniques copied from the ore-mining industries of driving levels into the hillside (see below) to intersect slate deposits deep underground. They were then worked as underground closeheads (left).

Nowadays most slate is obtained by open-cast quarrying techniques such as at Elterwater Quarry, shown here. All photos – A Cameron

expanded, they took on men as full time employees. Existing operations slowly followed suit. Eventually the Company system became a thing of the past.

Most of the quarries, especially the larger ones, required additional groups of employees. These included the miners or 'level-drivers' who were responsible for driving the tunnels forward until good slate 'metal' was located. They were normally paid by the distance (fathoms) of tunnel driven. Labourers worked in groups known as 'rids'. They were responsible for clearing the waste rock from the workings. Carters transported slate to Coniston station yard, smiths sharpened drill steels and hoisters operated the aerial ropeways. Since the Second World War the demand for roofing slates has fallen but the market for cladding has expanded considerably. These new markets have required many additional new skills.

In former years the spearhead of a quarry operation, the highly skilled people, were the quarrymen themselves who studied and worked the faces, handled the clogs into manageable pieces and the rivers and dressers who manufactured and completed the finished slates.

Traditionally there were two rockmen in a Company who would work the face. Prior to the development of the use of gunpowder in about 1760, blocks of slate would be taken from the face by hand, making use of the natural fissures in the rock. As soon as explosives became available a whole new skill developed involving the careful boring of shot-holes into which the explosive powder was inserted. Hand boring of a shot hole usually involved two men. One would hold the heavy drill, known as a jumper, while the other struck it using a heavy long handled hammer. As the end of the drill was struck the one holding it would rotate it about a third of a turn so that, as well as the force of the impact, a shearing action in the turning of the drill head helped in the progress of operation. Hand boring a shot hole was an extremely skilled operation. It was important to drive the drill in a straight line to avoid it becoming jammed and difficult to remove. There was also a tendency to create a pinnacle of rock right at the end of the hole which the drill head would orbit around as the hole was driven further. This resulted in an enlarged hole which would not necessarily produce the best results on blasting. Avoiding this was known, at Coniston, as "keeping the lad out of the hole".

There are surprisingly few records of injuries to hands resulting from hand boring. In fact it appears to have been one of the safer operations in slate extraction. One was much more likely to be hit on the head by a stone falling from the closehead roof than to have one's wrists smashed by a mate's mis-placed hammer stroke.

With the introduction of compressed air rock drills at the end of the 19th Century levels could be driven and faces worked much more quickly. But in some of the more remote workings high on the fells, hand boring continued for many years, in fact it was still being practised well within living memory.

The size of the blocks that rockmen produced was most important. Later handling required a particular size with the bate running the correct way. It was also essential to reduce to a minimum the small fragments that broke off in order to prevent wastage. Rockmen would stand for hours discussing the best position to site shotholes and how they should be fired. They would study the line of cleavage, any fissures in the area being worked and use them to the best advantage. They would also consider the layout of the face for future blasts. This was highly skilled work requiring years of experience.

The same is true today. In the open-top quarries the same care and planning goes into working a face as it did hundreds of years ago. Traditional gunpowder is still used instead of gelignite as the shattering effect is much less. The introduction of large machines has, however, produced major changes in the operation of quarries. In the old days, an error in the placing of a charge could result in many weeks of work clearing the debris from the quarry floor using the traditional corrack and tub. The quarry could be out of operation for much of this time. Today large mechanical shovels can clear debris in a fraction of the time.

Rockmen have several blasting techniques available to them. The most simple and the most frequently used in past years, is where a piece of rock can be brought down by drilling a few shot holes and inserting powder and a fuse. In the greenslate quarries at Coniston, 'cross holes' were usually drilled across the direction of the 'bate'. Coniston's slate contained far more natural joints and seams than, say, the sedimentary slates of Kirkby and the drilling of cross holes allowed the rockmen to obtain better sized pieces of rock. In the sedimentary slate, holes were more often drilled along the direction of the bate. When the face being worked was in an underground closehead, the charges were usually set off right at the end of a working day. This allowed the chamber to clear of dust and fumes during the night.

Another technique which has been used occasionally at Coniston in the open-top workings is one known as 'springing the shothole'. This consists of drilling one or more holes with a heavy burden above. A succession of gradually increasing charges of gunpowder is detonated until the rock fractures, usually along a plane of weakness. Finally a large charge is made in the fracture which brings down the block. The advantage of this technique is that, normally, a high yield results with minimum wastage in the form of fragments.

The technique of springing is quite an art and the results depend to a great extent on the skills of the shotfirer. The decision to cease springing and apply the final blast is made by an experienced man who has been watching the quarry face very carefully during the latter stages of springing.

Yet another technique used from time to time is that of 'gryking' in which powder is poured down into the natural fissures in the rock behind the material to be dislodged. This is usually done along the top of the quarry face and frequently

117

in the region of 400 – 500 kilograms of powder is used. A fuse is then inserted down into the fissure and the charge set off. It is said that the ratio of rock brought down to quantity of powder used (known as the 'yield ratio') is high using this technique. Occasionally, if no natural fissures exist above the quarry face, these can be created by drilling a number of shotholes downwards behind the face to a depth of up to 50ft. The holes are charged with powder and stemmed with several feet of slate dust. If correctly calculated, the resulting charge will be sufficient to create suitable fractures for gryking, or alternatively, the whole face can be brought down in one operation. It was an advantage to leave some broken rock on the quarry floor to soften the impact caused by the fall.

One such gryking blast that will long be remembered in Coniston took place on Friday May 20th 1977. George Birkett was the quarry manager at Brossen Stone which was at that time being operated by Lakeland Green Slate Company. George supervised the careful placing of only 56lb of powder into natural cracks behind a large block of slate. A fuse was inserted and the powder ignited. Mike Brownlee, the managing director of the company, watched what happened. "*There was a bang and then for several seconds nothing happened. Then we heard a beautiful sliding sound like a ship being launched.*" Three hundred tons of slate in three huge blocks slid down the face and dropped twenty feet to the quarry floor. George, who had worked up on the Old Man since he was a boy, was convinced that they were the biggest blocks ever dislodged.

But the biggest bang of all, the "mother and father" of all detonations, must be that produced by the heading blast.

The basic idea of a heading blast is simple enough. It involves driving a tunnel or 'heading' for about 40 to 50ft into the face that is to be brought down, then turning through 90 degrees and continuing the drive for some distance along the back of the face. This final tunnel runs along the line of the 'bate' and is known as a 'bateway'. The bateway would be packed with up to ten tons of black powder explosive. The tunnel would then be sealed or 'stemmed' very thoroughly with walls of rock and the explosive would be fired by fuse. The resulting detonation would, in theory, blow the whole face forward.

In practice a considerable amount of skill and also a degree of luck were called for in siting the tunnel and packing the explosives in such a way that the explosion would make use of the natural planes of weakness of the rock and also the 'bate' of the slate. This was often assisted by cutting through the rock face using a wire saw to make an artificial fissure.

It must be said that, despite the skill of the quarrymen, and the use of wire saws, the heading blast was frequently unpredictable and since the mid 1980s the technique has been abandoned. The wastage level could be extremely high. Often many tons of slate would be shattered and end up on the tip.

The old timers claimed that heading blasts were introduced into Lakeland from the Furness limestone quarries. Preparation for a heading blast could take several months. The levels had to be driven and it usually took at least a week to undercut the face with a wire saw. Having done this it could take up to a fortnight to pack all the explosive and stem the areas where explosives had been sited. The final blast only took a few seconds, blowing the face forward, causing many thousands of tons of rock to pile up on the quarry floor and rattling the windows in Coniston and Torver. The demise of the "big shot" or "big blow" was partially caused by the cost of the explosive and the expense of the preparation work and partly by the unpredictability and the destruction of valuable slate rock. Heading blasts are now illegal.

Reports of failures of heading blasts are numerous. There was one "big shot" in a Langdale slate quarry which disgorged its stemming, blackened the opposite quarry face with a great smear of soot and frightened the life out of a group of campers in the valley below. And who would have stood in the boots of the shotfirer at Goldmire quarry in Low Furness, during the Second World War, as he watched his tunnel spitting fire and his meticulously packed stemming flying across the valley in the direction of a passing munitions train?

Brief mention has just been made of wire sawing. This technique is now very much in favour and is used universally in the area. The original type of wire sawing was the sand-wire saw. It was first developed and used in the Italian marble quarries of Carrara. It is said that it was introduced into the Cumbrian slate industry by Claude Cann, the quarryman of Cornish extraction whose success in locating slate on the fells above Torver is now legendary. The equipment consisted of an endless loop of wire driven via pulleys by an electric motor of approximately 15 hp. The wire was held against the rock by a number of ratchet tensioners. At the point at which the wire entered the cut in the rock, a sand-in-water slurry was fed onto it as a continuous flow. It was the sand as much as the wire itself which caused the cut. A wire sawing assembly was very flexible and could be installed at most points on the quarry face, provided that the plan of the area to be cut was convex.

Wire sawing revolutionised the extraction of slate. Wastage caused by heavy blasting which can be as high as 90%, was virtually eliminated. The rate of cutting through slate rock was about two inches an hour. The saw was left running day and night although the tensioners usually had to be re-positioned after the cut had advanced about 10ft. Other than that, and the fact that a saw wire was normally replaced after three days' use, the equipment could be left running by itself.

The sand-wire saws were phased out during the 1980s and replaced with the diamond-wire saw in which industrial diamonds are impregnated into the wire. The use of diamond-wire sawing was developed in the UK by the Lakeland Green

During archaeological work on Coniston Old Man in 2001, the remains of an ancient sledge track were discovered. It appears this track once ran from the Scald Cop workings, close to the summit, to Saddlestone lower down the mountain. More recent workings in the 18th and 19th centuries have obliterated much of the route but some parts still survive such as those shown in this photograph.

This strongly suggests that, during the Middle Ages, manufactured slates were removed from the working sites and transported down the mountain by sledge. Horses and carts were able to reach Saddlestone and slates were reloaded there for the journey down to the head of Coniston Lake.　　　　　　　　　　　　　　　　　　　　　　　　　　*Photo – A Cameron*

Slate Company following visits to marble quarries in Italy. They first used it at Bursting Stone Quarry. The wire travels at a phenomenal 60 mph and will cut approximately 6 square meters an hour. It is not necessary to use any abrasive and the only material which is fed onto the wire is water. Unlike the sand-wire saw which was normally pushed into a face, the diamond wire is pulled out of the face to be sawn, having previously been threaded through holes drilled with great accuracy through the back of the face.

The advantage of this type of sawing is that it is much quicker and leads to a more flexible operation. It is also cheaper and has a considerable effect on reducing waste even further.

As well as working a quarry face it is the responsibility of the rockmen to ensure that all loose blocks are removed so that those working the quarry floor are in no danger. The famous photograph of Jack Taylforth dislodging a loose block from the face at Broughton Moor with an iron bar while suspended by a heavy hemp rope was used by the Broughton Moor Company as a cover photograph for their sales literature.

As soon as a block is brought to the quarry floor it can be broken into more manageable sizes. In the underground closeheads, in former times, the size of a block could be no bigger than the dimensions of the access tunnel along which it had to be taken. If blocks had to be reduced in size this was frequently done by hand within the underground chambers using traditional techniques such as the 'hitch and dock' method with a large wooden mallet known as a 'mell' or by using a 'plug and feather'. The 'feather' is a form of circular, hollow, slightly tapered wedge which is in two halves. It is inserted into a hole drilled into the rock. The plug is a solid metal rod, also slightly tapered which is tapped home inside the feather causing a slight outward movement which splits the block. In practice, if the required split is to be along the line of the slate cleavage all that will be required will be to drill two or three holes to a depth of 6 to 10 inches into which the feather can be inserted. If splitting is to be done at right angles to the cleavage, a series of approximately 1¼ inch diameter holes are drilled at about 2¼ inch centres along the line of the intended fracture. Feathers are inserted in every third hole and the plugs driven home equally.

Today, from the open-top quarries, much bigger blocks can be handled and transported to the saw sheds by heavy vehicles. Plugs and feathers are still used occasionally but blocks are most frequently reduced using a technique known as channelling in which a series of closely spaced holes are drilled along the required line of splitting. More recently still, diamond-wire saws are used, with the wire wrapped round the block to be cut.

To transform a rough 'clog' into slate suitable to roof a building is yet another operation requiring a great deal of skill and experience. For generations Coniston quarrymen have practised the craft of riving, the art of splitting slates making use of the natural cleavage. This is a job which has hardly changed in the last three hundred years. In his book *The Old Man*, published in 1849, Gibson describes the rivers at work at Hodge Close Quarry a few miles to the north of Coniston:

> *"The clogs are thrown down in heaps at the open end of the shed, and are of various shapes and sizes, the average size being of a well-grown folio volume. These are riven into slate thickness by the river, who uses a hammer like a small pickaxe, with its point flattened and sharpened.*
> *The rivers stood in their open fronted sheds, deftly tapping at the slate. First they would dock unwanted corners from the clog with a tool called a 'tulley', a heavy hammer sharpened at one end like an axe. Then they would tap along the bate with the hammer like a small pickaxe (a riving hammer) gradually increasing the force of the blow until the clog splits. By repeating this again and again the required thickness was obtained. At this stage in the process the slates were called rivings and although thin enough, they were still rough round the edges. The river would then pass the slates to the 'dresser' who would complete the manufacturing process with his 'whittle and brake'.*
> *The dresser sits on a beam of wood into which is secured a long, flat topped staple (the brake). On the staple he holds the slates and chips them into shape (with the whittle). They are then laid aside and classified according to their fineness, the finest being called London, the second Country, the coarsest Tom, and a very small quality for slating the walls of houses is called a Peg."*

Techniques change slowly in the industry. Slate is still dressed in this manner though it is the exception rather than the rule; the majority of dressing is now done by machine. The work of the river however is largely the same, except that the Welsh method of splitting with a mallet and chisel has been adopted and the one time common-place riving hammer has been confined to antiquity. The skilled hammer rivers were masters of their craft. It has been said that a hammer river could produce a better quality slate than a mallet river, and from poorer rock as well. The Welsh method which requires less skill seems to have been introduced during the early years of the 20th Century. By the 1930s hammer rivers were a dying breed of men, all new apprentices were being instructed in the use of the mallet and chisel.

Gibson makes reference to the terminology used for different sizes of slate. This has changed somewhat over the years, and can also vary from location to location. In general at Coniston there were four classes of slates: London slates, Seconds, Thirds and Fourths. This seems to have taken over from the previous

London, Country and Toms. Depending on the quality of the rock at the quarry, the river would be able to produce a certain proportion of London slates but the rest would have to be lower quality ones.

The Lakeland slate industry was slow in adopting the use of mechanical sawing. In Wales the Greaves sawing table was first introduced in the 1850s and the formidable Hunter saw by the 1860s. There is a report that a crude timber-framed saw was in use at Blaenau Ffestiniog in 1802. It was only at the turn of the century that power saws were becoming extensively adopted in Lakeland. By the 1930s, however, diamond saws were coming into general use in all areas.

One aspect of the industry which relied heavily on sawing was the slab quarries, situated on Coniston's sedimentary slate beds. They produced their own range of products. Most of them published a product and price list which would usually include flooring slabs, sills, steps, lintels and a whole range of other items for building construction. All these needed to be cut by saw. In many cases, before the advent of circular saws, the stone had to be cut by hand using hand saws. The period between 1880 and 1910 were the boom years for the slab quarries and they were often much more profitable than their greenslate neighbours in the high fells. One of the biggest slab quarries in the Coniston area was the Banniside Quarry at Tranearth above Torver. It was not until the 1890s that The Coniston Slate Company, who operated Banniside, installed a water powered circular slab-cutting saw. Before then all stone was cut by hand.

Much of the slate rock which is handled today is destined for architectural work. This requires extremely accurate sawing to close tolerances and over the past few decades many types of saws have been installed by the large operators including up-to-the-minute laser-guided equipment. This type of technology, as in all areas, changes very rapidly. But forty years ago many extensive architectural contracts were completed using much more basic cutting equipment.

In 1958 the Lakeland Green Slate and Stone Company successfully completed the contract to supply cladding for the British Engine Insurance Building in Manchester. At the time it was the largest green-slate cladding contract ever awarded. At the Company's Moss Rigg Quarry rough slate blocks brought from the quarry face were initially sawn using a reciprocating frame saw. The hardened steel blades fitted into the saw frame gave about 200 strokes of 12 inches a minute. The blades were fed with a mixture of water, sand and hard steel shot to assist in the sawing. This saw produced rough slabs which were then passed to a rise and fall circular saw fitted with a 42" diameter diamond tipped blade that rotated at 750 rpm. There were a number of other saws in the sheds at Moss Rigg which were used for handling smaller pieces of work.

Cut slate which required polishing would be passed over to further skilled hands. The traditional 'Jenny Lind' polishing machine has been used for many years by the slate industry. It is fitted with a rise-and-fall head. Different grades of carborundum heads are used during the polishing operation; the final 'polish' is obtained using a revolving felt pad. The machine got its name from the fact that the perfect finish matched the voice of the Swedish singer of that name who was popular during the second half of the 19th Century. Modern slate processing plants now use diamond polishers and flow-line production techniques.

The transport of finished product away from the quarries frequently created problems for the slate companies. Unlike the industry in Wales, very little mechanisation was used with the exception of the Mandalls quarries on Coniston Old Man. Here a series of aerial flights were constructed to bring, initially, finished slates, but, ultimately, slate block down from the high working sites to collecting points from where it could be removed by road.

Many interesting comparisons can be made between the Welsh slate industry and that in Cumbria. In general the tonnages produced in Wales were much greater and much more mechanisation was to be seen by the end of the 19th Century. It was usual for Welsh quarries to construct large 'mills' close to the quarries in which all processing equipment was installed under one roof. Finished product would be dispatched directly from the mills. Because of the scale of operations Welsh slate quarries soon found themselves unable to compete unless they could install a rail link from the quarry to the coast or valley rail-head. These were usually of the narrow gauge type. At Coniston none of the quarries had such luxury, although it was occasionally discussed. Until road vehicles were introduced, all transport from the quarry to Coniston or Torver station yards was by horse and cart. Often a sledge would be dragged behind the cart on steep descents such as from the Old Man Quarries to Coniston station. This served two purposes, it would increase the quantity that could be carried and also act as a brake during the steep descent to Coniston. The quarry owners considered this a good idea. Not so Coniston Parish Council, who frequently complained about the state of the roads on which sledges were used.

In more recent times most of the major quarries such as Brossen Stone, Broughton Moor and Moss Rigg had their own processing sheds on the quarry bank. Product would be delivered directly from there by road vehicle. Within the past twenty years however, things have changed and the industry has concentrated on centralising processing at one site at Kirkby, outside the restrictive confines of the Lake District National Park. All slate clog from the Coniston quarries is now taken down the valley by truck to be processed there.

GAZETTEER

In this section the majority of the quarry workings on the fells and within the woods around Coniston village will be described. This section is primarily intended to document the workings for industrial archeological purposes. But there is a very great fascination in old remains amongst those who are familiar with and walk on the Coniston Fells and it is hoped that the descriptions that follow will be of interest to them as well. Many of the workings are on private property with no public access. Permission should always be sought before a visit. Some workings include extensive areas that are underground. It is recommended that would-be explorers do not venture into these areas without expert guidance and full equipment. All underground slate workings are potentially very dangerous.

The slate workings have been divided into five geographical sections:

> Torver quarries including Gold Scope
> Quarries on Coniston Old Man
> Quarries in the Coppermines Valley
> Tilberthwaite quarries
> Coniston's slab quarries

Intentionally, little if any reference is made to those quarries that are currently in operation. It is essential that these areas are not encroached upon. In future years it is very likely that some workings that are at the moment abandoned and included in this book, may be re-opened and if this is the case these should be treated with the same respect.

TORVER QUARRIES

Ash Gill Quarry
SD269954

The rough stony track leaves Torver village for Ash Gill at Under Crag and climbs steeply up the bank to the top. Beyond, the fell opens out. The track crosses the lonely and wet moorland and eventually arrives at the quarry. It was down this track that carts laden with slate from Ash Gill trundled en route to Torver station yard. The last cart load of slate was carried down by Harold Grisedale in 1925.

This route is not recommended today. Anyone wishing to explore Ash Gill and the surroundings will find the route via Tranearth much more pleasant. The workings lie on either side of Ash Gill Beck and consist of a number of open pits some of which had been worked previously as closeheads. Ash Gill lies close to the band of Coniston Limestone and the area of the quarry has been a favourite haunt of fossil collectors over the years. It was predominantly a slab quarry working the sedimentary slates but there is some suggestion that the quarry also

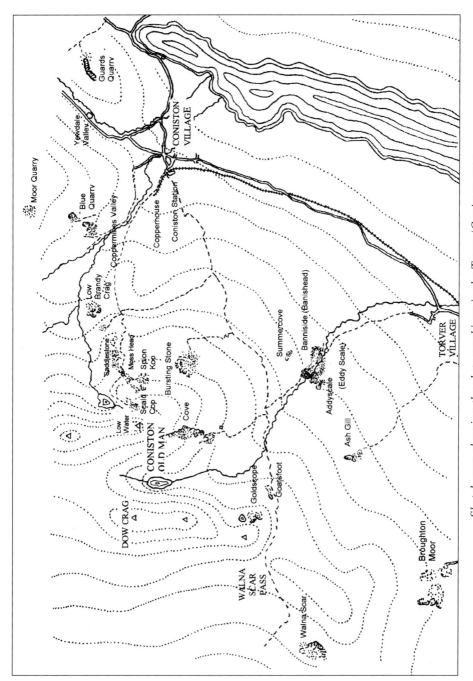

Sketch map showing the slate workings in the Torver/Coniston area

worked pockets of volcanic slate which, if it was the case, must have been part of the light green slate band. Certainly the areas of dressing waste on the tips seem to confirm this. At the northern end of the quarry a large shallow pit has been formed from slate working. Here the main problem which affected the quarry can be seen very clearly. Much of the slate is impregnated with impurities giving it an extremely 'rusty' appearance. It was not the easiest area to work and did not produce significant returns during the 20th Century.

The quarry probably started working in the early 1700s. As it was not on manorial land there are few records in the archives to consult for historical data. However by 1850 the quarry was extensive and there are stories locally that, before the railway opened, slate was carted directly from the quarry over Broughton Moor and down past Appletree Worth Farm to the coast on the Duddon Sands for shipment away. The quarry grew in size over the next fifty years, which were the boom years for slab production. The 1912 edition of the Ordnance Survey map shows the quarry as being disused although this is certainly not correct. The last proprietor was Casson Brocklebank who, it is reputed, lived up at the quarry and probably worked it alone, bringing in assistance when required.

The foundations of a few buildings remain, some of which appear to have been dressing sheds. We do not know whether any mechanical saws were installed and it is possible that all sawing of slabs was done by hand right up to the end. Right beside the beck a level runs into the bank, but this soon opens out into a pit quarry and therefore is not worth the effort to explore. On a warm summer's day when the more popular parts of the fells are thronged with walkers, Ash Gill can provide a haven of peace to settle down and read the Sunday papers.

Tranearth Slab Quarries
SD279959

The three quarries at Tranearth started at a much later date than those at Ash Gill. All worked sedimentary slate except for a few outcrop workings on Flask Brow nearby which worked a narrow bed of Stockdale Shales on an experimental basis. In 1850 the Banniside Quarry, on the north east side of Torver Beck, was only very small but the Summercove working further over the moor to the east was producing commercial quantities. On the opposite side of the beck the Addyscale Quarry had started but had not developed to any extent. In 1863 the Cove and Banniside Slate Company started working Banniside Quarry and continued to do so until the end of the century. Their fortunes are recounted in the chapter '18th Century'. By this time the Flask Brow workings had closed down. The attempt to work the Stockdale Shales had not been successful. The Summercove workings had also closed by 1860.

The Mandall Company worked the Addyscale Quarry during the latter years of the 19th Century.

By 1890 both Addyscale and Banniside quarries had developed to something near present-day size. An open-topping operation had taken place at Banniside in 1872 with the underground closehead being converted to an open pit. For some reason the quarry names appear to have changed towards the end of the century to 'Eddy Scale' and 'Banishead' possibly due to yet another mistake by the Ordnance Survey. For the purpose of this description the original names will be retained.

In 1910 the Addyscale Quarry had run down but the Banniside workings continued to operate but required constant pumping to remove water. By the 1920s the quarry had closed. The market for flags had collapsed and the quarry pit had been extended dangerously close to the beck. Only a sturdy retaining wall prevented the water pouring into the quarry. Nothing happened at Banniside until 1959 when two local children decided to see what would happen if the retaining wall between the quarry and beck was demolished. They managed to break the wall down creating a magnificent waterfall (and nearly drowning themselves in the process). It took several days for the water level to rise to the lowest drainage point, which was the access tunnel out of which most of the contents of the beck now started to flow, much to the farmer's annoyance. The resulting waterfall is still pouring into the quarry.

The route from Torver to these quarries starts from the Scar Head road end just to the north of the village. The cart track runs through the collection of houses and then climbs the bank to open out onto the moorland. A short distance further on the quarries are seen ahead. Nearby is Tranearth Farm, now a climbing centre owned by the Lancashire Caving and Climbing Club.

At Tranearth the original route crossed Torver Beck by a ford which, after periods of heavy rain, required constant attention when the quarries were operating. Today a bridge crosses the beck higher up. The main bank of Banniside quarry can be seen ahead. On the other side of the beck the spoil banks of Addyscale encroach right up to the beck. From the debris in the tips of both quarries one can get a good idea of the poor nature of the rock. The cart track climbs beside the large tip. At the top a number of ruined buildings were possibly for accommodation and just beyond is the cutting to the level entrance. The level was driven in 1872. Most of the product of the quarry came out of here. Somewhere in this area the proprietors installed their water-powered slab saw in 1871, but no signs of the installation survive.

Formerly rail tracks running along the level would have lead directly out on to the top of the main bank where there are the remains of a number of buildings and possibly a loading wharf. A line of derelict riving sheds are further along the top of the tip. Towards the end of the tip is another collection of derelict buildings one of which may have contained a blacksmith's hearth.

Beyond the entrance to the level the track climbs further and eventually reaches the rim of the main pit. The grassy tips just before the rim consist of material removed from the roof during the open-topping operation in 1872. Apart from a few spikes sticking up out of the turf nothing remains of the hoisting arrangement used to raise stone from the quarry floor after the roof was removed. The rock in the walls of the pit shows very clearly the lie of the slate beds. From the rim the Summercove quarries can be seen across the moor to the north-west.

The Summercove workings are much smaller. A number of surface outcrops have been worked as small quarries. One must have appeared promising because, subsequently, a level was driven from lower down the fellside for about 60 meters to intersect the workings at a lower depth. This was then worked upwards to break through eventually to the surface. The level is now flooded and the author once waded up it coming back out to daylight in the base of the pit. The achievement hardly warranted the effort involved.

From the surface remains today it appears that the Summercove workings are very old. It is possible that slabs were being obtained from here well before 1800. The 1850 edition of the Ordnance Survey shows the workings not much smaller than they are today.

Addyscale Quarries are much more difficult to interpret than Banniside and at least five different pit workings seem to have been in operation over the years. Each pit would have commenced as an underground closehead, reached by a level. The Mandall Company ran Addyscale for some time and installed a water powered saw in July 1870. This caused an argument between Mandalls and their neighbours on the other side of Torver Beck. Mandalls had diverted about half of the flow of the beck to drive the wheel. The Cove and Banniside Company objected strongly to the le Fleming estate saying that they were concerned about the fishing in the river lower down. There was little the estate could do because Addyscale was not on their Manorial land. The real cause of the Company's concern was probably nothing to do with the fish. It was more likely the fact that they were planning to install their own wheel and were also hoping to use water from the beck as the source of power.

There are the remains of a few ruined buildings at Addyscale many of which could have been riving sheds. The entrances to the levels serving the pits are now completely run-in.

Throughout the life of both Addyscale and Banniside Quarries roofing slate was produced in addition to slabs. The quality of the slates was very poor. C M Jopling, in his *Sketch of Furness and Cartmel* refers to the fact that Addyscale Quarry was responsible for the poor reputation that Torver slate seemed to have in general. The beds of slate varied between flaggy and cleavable. There is a story still told today concerning the building of a house at Scar Head for John Barrett, proprietor of the Coniston Mine. Mr Barrett specified that the house, Crook House, should be roofed in Banniside slate. This was done as he requested but unfortunately, shortly after it was finished, it had to be completely re-roofed in slate from one of the higher greenslate quarries because the original slates had cracked and corroded. Even slabs, cills and walling stone produced at Tranearth were often of dubious quality.

Goatsfoot Quarries
SD265964

Goatsfoot Quarry, at the foot of the Walna Scar Pass, was opened during the 1820s. Access to the quarry was via the Walna Scar Road and the small amount of slate worked there would have been taken away by horse and cart. The quarry was working in 1850 but would not have survived long after that. Today little remains. A short level runs into the hill and this has been opened out to the surface. To the right of the level are the ruins of a riving shed and another building on the left may have been a cabin. There is another small working higher up to the south west. Goatsfoot worked the silver-grey band. The quarry has little claim to fame apart from the fact that the famous Victorian climber, W P Haskett-Smith ('father' of Lakeland mountaineering) climbed the quarry face on a day in April 1886 because he lost his way to Dow Crag in the mist.

Gold Scope Quarries
SD262966

Two tracks leave the Walna Scar Road and traverse the side of Brown Pike. The lower one serves the main Gold Scope Quarry and the higher one a smaller working slightly to the south. The route to the higher working appears to have been a pony track. The higher workings themselves are on the steep mountainside and were possibly partly underground with the level now completely run-in. There is too much rubbish on the hillside below to be from the open workings alone. A ruined building at the entrance to the level appears to be a cabin with an adjacent riving shed. Very little is known about the history of this particular site.

The lower track from the Walna Scar Road leads to the main Gold Scope workings. The track skirts below the main bank and then swings sharply round to the left and climbs steeply up on to it. On the main bank is a large number of ruined buildings of various sizes with one building still possessing a roof. There are some large stacks of stone and the remains of a smithy. The entrance to the underground areas are just behind the buildings. Further along the bank, to the north, a considerable proportion of the face has been worked away. Further round still, the remains of a large cabin are perched on the edge of a drop. Behind this cabin a level formerly ran into the hill but the entrance is now completely blocked.

Gold Scope worked a band of dark grey slate. The only other quarry to work this band was at Common Wood in the Duddon Valley. The slate was very hard and difficult to rive.

The quarries here, just below the summit of Brown Pike, were one of the very first to be worked on the Coniston Fells. In 1680 they were well established and could have been working for over one hundred years before this date. The quarries were not on any manorial lands and therefore few records exist. The last proprietor was Gordon Kendal who worked the quarry until the 1920s. Details of the exploits by him and his father are given on page 47.

QUARRIES ON CONISTON OLD MAN

Cove Quarry
SD272972-5

This high and extensive working on the silver-grey band has its origin well before 1700. It extends up the south west flank of Coniston Old Man and was worked in roughly three sections, High, Middle and Low Cove. It is likely that the first workings, which are now largely obliterated, would have been at Middle or High Cove where the slate band clearly outcrops. Over the centuries much work has concentrated on Middle Cove where the once-underground chambers have been opened out. At Low Cove the workings are predominantly in closeheads. They are on gently sloping ground and several have collapsed with tell-tale depressions in the fell side indicating where chamber roofs have fallen in. The High Cove workings are on extremely steep exposed ground at an altitude approaching 2000ft. Much of the quarrying here during the 19th Century was purely face-working.

The land on which Cove is situated formed part of the Manor of Coniston. Cove features extensively in much of the le Fleming archive material. This is described in the section dealing with the exploits of the Coniston Slate Company on page 36.

Remains today are quite extensive although the site has been badly affected by the weather. The most impressive remnant is the relatively recent access road that winds through the lower workings up to High Cove. This was designed to take horses and carts and has been extremely well engineered. In the 1890s, during the period when the Coniston Slate Company re-established High Cove, the road was improved and has over-ridden older remains. Transport from Cove was always a problem. Pack ponies would have been used before the cart road was constructed and the quarry never progressed further than the horse-and-cart era, right up to when the last work was done there in the late 1920s. One of the last carters was Harold Grisedale of Coniston, who was in the employ of Cornish entrepreneur, Claude Cann.

This photograph is very old and slightly faded but nevertheless shows an important scene. The location is some way down the Old Man quarry road where two slate carts each towing a sledge on wheels have come to a halt. The wheels, or paddocks, were removable and were left behind when the cart reached the top of Coniston Station Hill. The sledge then acted as a brake on the descent towards the village. At Coniston station iron rollers under each load helped the horse pull the sledge onto the loading wharf. On the return trip up to the quarries the sledges were loaded well forward in the carts and the paddock collected on the way.

Photo – Ruskin Museum archives

132

The route of the cart track can be traced from the Walna Scar Road. It follows the present day climber's track to Dow Crag for a few hundred meters and then swings away to the right to climb up to the quarry. En route the road passes close to the derelict remains of the powder magazine which was built a healthy distance away from the workings. After the quarries closed this building was taken over by local climbers and was used for many years for overnight accommodation. It is said that it was the first 'climber's hut' in the Lake District and has had an interesting and colourful history which is well documented in climbing literature.

From the powder magazine the line of workings above are quite obvious and show the lie of the slate bed very clearly. On the main bank at Low Cove are the remains of a number of buildings. One, which is still in use, is the Jack Diamond Memorial Hut named after a Coniston schoolmaster who was a keen mountaineer. Attached is a derelict building which appears to have been a stable. Close behind the hut a level runs into the hill. This is now blocked. A building which no longer exists (but is marked on the old quarry plans of 1910) is the straw-house directly above Jack Diamond's Hut. This was where powder straws were stored.

Above is the main bank of Middle Cove which is quite large. On it are the remains of a number of riving sheds and stone cabins. The bank served a large quarry which was opened out from a closehead in the 1860s. Today the quarry has been partially filled with rid from workings above. At the back, the quarry runs into an ancient closehead which must pre-date the open workings by well over 100 years.

Slightly higher a pit working is accessed by a blocked level. This has also been used for tipping from above. In this area the construction of the cart road is quite impressive. The uppermost part of Middle Cove was worked from an underground chamber. The access level shows an excellent example of 'Matt Spedding' tunnelling which appears to enter the hill from the back of a building. This level is open and is one of the very few examples of this type of tunnelling in the slate workings on the Old Man. There are some extremely interesting remains in this area including a smithy. The crag above has been worked at a very early date. Could this be the site of the workings of the late 1600s? An in-depth study by industrial historians with a keen eye is required here. The highest quarry in Middle Cove was one of the last areas worked.

From Middle Cove the cart track continues to the upper quarry. Upper Cove consists of little more than a series of open workings that have sliced into the mountain. All remains of the entrances to the underground chambers of the 18th Century have been run-in. It is very unlikely that these underground workings, just beneath the summit of the mountain, will ever be entered again. The open workings are at an acute angle. At the top of Upper Cove the face severely overhangs the quarry floor. This must have presented great difficulties to the

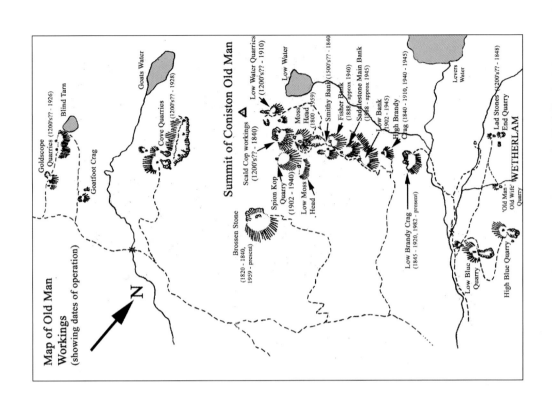

Map of Old Man Workings
(showing dates of operation)

Summit of Coniston Old Man

Goldscope Quarries (1200's?? - 1926)
Blind Tarn
Goatfoot Crag
Goats Water
Cove Quarries (1200's?? - 1928)
Low Water Quarries (1200's?? - 1910)
Scald Cop workings (1200's?? - 1840)
Low Water
Moss Head (1800 - 1959)
Smithy Bank (1500's?? - 1840)
Fisher Bank (1888 - approx 1940)
Saddlestone Main Bank (1888 - approx 1945)
Low Bank 1902 - 1945)
High Brandy Crag (1840 - 1910, 1940 - 1945)
Spion Kop Quarry (1902 - 1940)
Low Moss Head
Brossen Stone (1820 - 1840, 1959 - present)
Low Brandy Crag (1845 - 1920, 1982 - present)
Levers Water
Lad Stones (1200's?? - 1848)
End Quarry
WETHERLAM
'Old Man' 'Old Wife' Quarry
Low Blue Quarry
High Blue Quarry

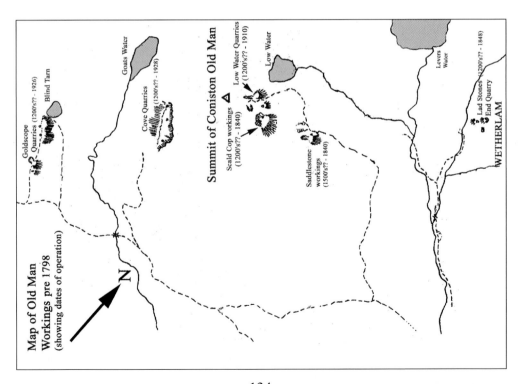

Map of Old Man Workings pre 1798
(showing dates of operation)

Summit of Coniston Old Man

Goldscope Quarries (1200's?? - 1926)
Blind Tarn
Goats Water
Cove Quarries (1200's?? - 1928)
Low Water Quarries (1200's?? - 1910)
Scald Cop workings (1200's?? - 1840)
Low Water
Saddlestone workings (1500's?? - 1840)
Levers Water
Lad Stones (1200's?? - 1848)
End Quarry
WETHERLAM

134

Coniston Slate Company when they worked here in the 1890s. A dressing shed in a remarkably exposed location has views right across the fells beyond Morecambe Bay to the Yorkshire Dales. This must be a good contender for the 'dressing shed with the finest view in Lakeland'.

The highest workings at Cove consist of little more than small trials into the band with the remains of a few stone buttresses and walls which were no doubt an attempt to create some level ground for working.

Many years ago, while at school in Coniston, the writer remembers the stories that were told of walking through the mountain from the Old Man Quarries to Cove. In reality it is very unlikely that this was ever possible. The distances are quite great and, in practice, there would have been no need to connect the two operations. There are many examples in similar research in various parts of the world of this type of claim. Normally they are found to be unsubstantiated.

Cove Quarries are well worth a visit. But those who do so should be competent fell walkers and have good footwear. They should keep clear of the extremely exposed places. When wet, the slate rivings underfoot become very slippery. Stay away when the mist is down or it is raining.

Old Man Quarries
SD276979-282982

The remains of these workings up the north east side of Coniston Old Man are extensive, a reflection of their past prosperity. Many village families have had past connections with working at these quarries. The route from Coniston through the quarries is one of the most popular walker's routes to the top of the mountain. Although most of the remains which the route passes are from the past 140 years, there are some much earlier workings which have, up to now, received little attention from archaeologists. The description that follows is given in the order of the ascent, so that those who feel energetic enough to do the climb can use it to add interest. Most walkers start from the car park at the former Coniston station or take their cars up to the Walna Scar fell gate at the end of the surfaced road.

From the fell gate at SD289971 the right hand track is the old quarry road along which, each morning, lorries used to wind their way up to the quarries carrying the quarrymen to work. This was also the route for slate down to Coniston station. In former times slate was carted down with each cart dragging a sledge behind it. The sledge would carry extra slate and also act as a brake on the steep descent to Coniston station. On the less steep section from the quarry to the top of the Station Hill the sledge would run on its own set of wheels which resembled a flat trolley or 'paddock'. This would be left behind at the top of the steep section. For the rest of the journey down to Coniston station the sledge was dragged on its runners. The road was a public highway and the state of the surface was a constant

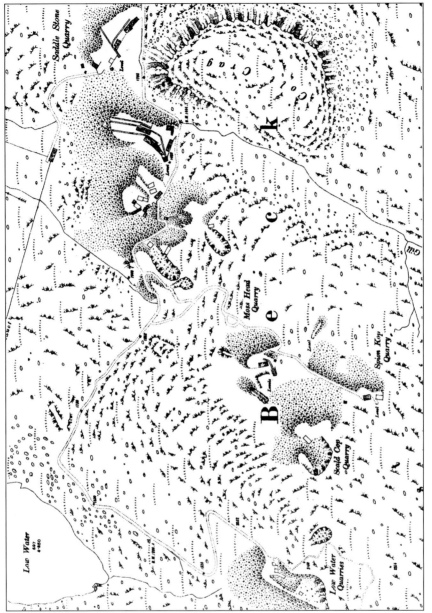

This section of the 1915 Ordnance Survey shows the layout of the Old Man Quarries as they were at the start of the 20th Century. The area covers Low Bank (labelled as Saddle Stone Quarry on the map) up to Low Water Quarries. The main production areas in the lower half of the works, Low Bank, Saddle Stone and Smithy Bank, are all well developed. Further up the mountain the Moss Head site is beginning to be developed. Between the two the ancient cave workings at 'Light Hole' and Fisher Bank are also marked although the former site is destined to become much larger over the next thirty years.

After many hundred years of operation both ancient workings of Scald Cop and Low Water were hardly being worked at all in 1915, but the new Spion Kop development was beginning to take shape.

It is interesting that the aerial flight from Spion Kop to Stubbthwaite Moss is not marked on the map although by 1915 it was clearly in place. However the Smithy has been built at the base of the Saddlestone Bank and part of the pen-stock (down pipe) from Low Water Tarn is also shown.

136

problem to the Coniston Parish Council at the turn of the century. The quarry owners were totally indifferent to their requests to stop using sledges.

Approximately 800 meters along the track from the fell gate the hillside on the left opens out into the marshy depression of Stubthwaite Moss. This was once the bottom terminus of the Spion Kop ropeway. Wooden stagings constructed on the Moss held finished slates ready for carting down to the village. On clear days the remains of the ropeway supports can be seen running up the hillside above.

Beyond Stubthwaite Moss the quarry road continues on and soon swings sharply round to the left, behind a small hill. At this point the Coppermines Valley can be seen below on the right, and a track climbing out of the valley joins the quarry road. This was once the path used by the quarrymen to walk to and from work before road transport was introduced after the Second World War. Fifty meters further on a cart track branches off on the left. It leads to the High Brandy Crag quarry where slate from higher workings was once processed after being lowered down from the Saddlestone bank on an aerial hoist.

The first quarry bank to be reached is Low Bank. There are few remains left on the bank itself and the level which formerly ran into the hill to access the silver-grey band is now completely run-in. It is unfortunate that the Low Bank level cannot be accessed because a branch of the level entered and worked an area of 'white' slate. It was known as White Quarry and the slate resembled a form of mica and could be rived extremely thinly. Another branch of the level entered Grey Quarry. Low Bank supported two Companies of men in the years up to the Second World War including two notable Coniston quarrymen, Jack Taylforth and George Brownlee.

The quarry road continues its climb past Low Bank to reach Saddlestone. For many years this was the main processing area for the quarries. Slate clog from workings above was carried down here on the aerial flights. Remains of the ropeway down from Moss Head above can be seen and also the office and saw shed. Mandalls installed a fixed-height utility saw here in 1938. It had been bought from Bramley Engineering in Leeds and was powered by an electric motor. It had a 41" diameter steel blade with a carborundum rim and could cut clogs up to 14" thick.

Slate clogs descending on the aerial flight would land on rail bogies and be taken into the shed. They would then be lifted from the bogies by block and tackle and lowered onto the saw table. The table, mounted on rails, was wound manually into the saw, the rate of travel being governed by the skill of the operator. Old photographs of the Saddlestone bank show a number of riving sheds and small workshops.

The bank is quite extensive and it is interesting to find off-cuts of light green slate amongst the silver-grey. The sharp eyed will also spot pieces of white slate in places. It is assumed that the light green came from Brossen Stone Quarry during the early years of its development while the white slate would have been brought up from Low Bank below.

From the edge of the bank, overlooking the Coppermines valley, remains of the 'smithy' can be seen below. This was the power house for the quarries and generated electricity and compressed air. It also contained a blacksmith's hearth. The power source was a pelton wheel fed by a water pipe from Low Water tarn. The wheel drove, by a series of belts, a single stage air compressor, a generator and also a pedestal drilling machine. An air receiver was installed which delivered air up to all the Saddlestone levels as well as to Moss Head and Spion Kop high above. The supply of air from the smithy was supplemented by air piped up from a compressor in the Coppermines Valley which was coupled into the air receiver.

The quarry road climbs up above the Saddlestone bank. In the corner below the road, as it leaves the bank, is the site of the entrance of the Saddlestone level. Until recently it was badly run-in. In 1994 a group of industrial archaeologists opened the level and explored the underground areas. They found a tunnel approximately 200ft long leading to a large closehead. A massive collapse of rock from the closehead roof filled most of the chamber. The internal areas were photographed and the explorers left. The level has now been effectively re-sealed.

A short distance above the Saddlestone bank the road arrives at Smithy Bank. The level here was driven in the late 1880s, at the same time as the Saddlestone level below. A number of buildings remain, one of which had been a riving shed. The level is open and leads to a closehead. A collapse from the roof has blocked most of the chamber.

Further up the mountainside is the large open pit, the lower part of which was being worked within living memory. It is believed that Smithy Bank closehead broke out into the base of the pit and debris falling from above eventually blocked the whole closehead.

Old plans show that the chambers at the end of the levels below Smithy Bank were interlinked by roofing shafts. It is likely that the debris in the Saddlestone closehead below could well have originated from Smithy Bank above.

The old quarry road climbs above Smithy Bank to reach the ancient workings of Fisher Bank. Ahead is a collapsed pylon of the aerial flight with its heavy static ropes draped up the mountainside. Nearby fencing has been installed by the land-owners. Just below is the entrance to a level. The portal consists of an attractive masonry arch. Much of the accessible tunnel inside is arched in a similar manner. This is a most unusual feature for slate workings. The author knows of no other such arching in the Coniston slate area. It is clearly very old. After a few feet the tunnel swings sharply round to the right and the way forward is then blocked by a collapse from the roof. The tunnel has been extended forward several times over the years.

138

On the surface it is possible to plot the direction the tunnel would have taken and its ultimate destination. It is quite obvious that it runs into some old workings above and to the right. These are part of the original Saddlestone workings, considered by Wilson in his survey of 1792 as only having '*middling prospects*' because they were '*rubbished up*' although the quality of the slate was '*fine*'. This was one of the very first areas of extraction on Coniston Old Man and a careful archeological survey is required here.

Just beyond the pylon are the remains of a building which had a fireplace in the back wall. The author has always assumed that this was an old smithy, but he has no real evidence to back this up. To the right of the building the narrow cutting runs directly into a partly roofed closehead, part of the ancient Saddlestone workings mentioned above.

From close to the pylon an old track to the right leads up to the lip of the large pit. The origins of these workings are again pre-1800 but a considerable amount of slate has been removed by more recent operations. This area was referred to by quarrymen as Light Hole. The upper part of the pit was once roofed over; effectively it was a closehead chambered out to the surface. One night during the 1940s the whole closehead collapsed, the roof caving in along the line of the 'slipe' that formed the southern wall. Although the collapse inundated the workings on Fisher Bank below, slate extraction continued as an open-top operation. Further to the right, along the edge of the pit, are the remains of the upper end of the short aerial flight that carried clogs down to the main bank below.

Above the Saddlestone workings the tips of Moss Head and Spion Kop cascade down the mountain and spill over into the open pit. Access to Moss Head is best done from near the shore of Low Water by striking across the mountain-side, although, formerly, it could be reached by a cart track from Smithy Bank.

On the top of the main bank at Moss Head is a considerable quantity of debris from the middle decades of the 20th Century. The upper terminus of the Moss Head Ropeway was sited here as was also the terminus for a blondin hoist which brought slate clog up from Moss Head Low Level to the bank. The main support for the former was a steel pylon which has now toppled over. The latter was supported by a series of wooden poles which are still standing.

The main Moss Head Ropeway was self-activating. The presence of an air-operated winch might therefore seem slightly puzzling. However the reason for it is simple. It was installed to assist the ropeway because, on occasions, material would be loaded onto the returning ropeway cradles at the lower Moss Head Middle Level and both sides of the ropeway would then carry the same weight. The winch was required to enable the cradles to complete the journey.

The blondin hoist on the bank was also powered by an air-operated winch. It was installed after the Spion Kop ropeway was abandoned.

This water balance lift was installed at Hodge Close around the turn of the century. Water balances were used in a number of quarries in the area and worked on the principle that the weight of a heavy tank of water descending on one set of guide rails would be sufficient to raise slate clog on the other set of rails. At Hodge Close this water balance did not raise slate right up to the quarry rim but only to a point midway up, from where it was trammed along a tunnel to exit some distance down the hillside.

This water balance lift was not used for many years. It suffered badly from damage by rock-falls from the sides of the quarry and, as the floor of the quarry was worked downwards, proved very inflexible. It was replaced by the blondin crane.   *Photo – Ruskin Museum archives*

Right on the edge of the bank at Moss Head is a stone cabin containing a sheave wheel and brake drum. The hoister would stand in the cabin and look out of the window down the length of the ropeway. The cabin was some distance in front of the main ropeway sheave wheel which was sited behind the top pylon. The travelling rope ran round the main wheel at the back of the bank then forward to the wheel in the brake cabin. This arrangement allowed the hoister (who in later years would be George Coward, the quarry foreman) to control the operation of the ropeway much more effectively because he could see exactly what was happening below.

The level into the mountain from Moss Head is open but should not be entered by those not fully equipped and unfamiliar with the area. The level leads, eventually, to the substantial chamber formed when the closeheads of Moss Head Middle and Upper levels broke into the Spion Kop complex above and became one.

Just below the main bank, to the south, is the Moss Head Middle Level bank. An old secondary air receiver lies in the cutting to the level mouth. Middle Moss Head was the very last area worked at the Old Man Quarries. A few months after closure the Lakeland Company received an order for large sized slates. About five quarrymen went back to take material out of Middle Moss Head closehead. They put in a shot bringing down a quantity of rock from which they selected the very best pieces and left the rest. The remaining clogs are still there. Fortunately the blondin up to High Moss Head was still in working order as was the aerial flight down to Saddlestone.

Further to the south, and slightly lower, is the site of the Moss Head Low Level. Formerly finished slate from here was carried on a rail track across the hillside to a point under the Spion Kop ropeway. Remains of the track can be followed today. More recently slate clog was raised by the blondin hoist up to the main Moss Head bank. The level from Low Moss Head runs into a closehead which has not become connected underground with any other part of the Moss Head system. This was the sad scene of the discovery of a suicide victim during the winter of 2003/4.

Above Moss Head are the ancient workings of Scald Cop. On the mountainside, between the two, are the remains of what appears to be an old sledging route in a remarkably good condition. It seems very likely that slate from Scald Cop was taken down to Saddlestone this way. Having delivered his load, the sledge-man would then have to climb back to Scald Cop with the empty sledge. It is interesting to see that adjacent to the sledge route are the remains of a well graded ziz-zag path which may have been constructed for this purpose.

Scald Cop was one of the earliest sites of extraction at Coniston. It is very likely that slate was worked here in the early 1600s. In 1792 Wilson described

Scald Cop as being 'badly rubbished up' but worthy of future investment. The 1860 map shows the workings in operation but by 1890 they had closed down.

On the main bank at Scald Cop are the remains of a few buildings, one of which may have been a stables. The level into the underground workings runs in from the back of the main open quarry. These ancient underground workings are in a very unstable condition. On no account should they be entered.

The last working on this side of the mountain was only established in 1902. Below Scald Cop and a little way to the south the Spion Kop workings were developed by driving a relatively long tunnel through country rock to intersect the slate band some way into the mountain. There were several reasons for doing this, one being the fact that tipping waste rock from the new quarry would not encroach on workings below. The history of the development of Spion Kop is described on page 48.

The causeway linking Moss Head with Spion Kop is still accessible today. It leads to the main Spion Kop bank at the point where the head of the aerial flight down to Stubthwaite Moss was sited. The ropeway was powered by gravity and worked for over 40 years. There are a number of derelict buildings on the bank one of which was a saw house. The Mandall Company installed an electric saw here in the 1920s. It was seated on a concrete bed, the remains of which can still be seen today. Slate clogs from the underground areas were trammed directly to the saw house where they were hoisted onto the saw table by a chain and pulley block mounted on a high beam. Sawing the clogs prior to riving greatly reduced the wastage that occurred when blocks were split by hand.

The processing area at Spion Kop closed when the underground closeheads connected up. The saw was removed and buildings abandoned. There are still a number of slate clogs stacked on the bank which were the very last to be taken out of the level, but which never quite made the saw.

Low Water Quarries
SD274979
These most interesting and ancient workings are some of the earliest quarries to have been worked in Lakeland. They are situated on the steep northern face of the mountain above the combe holding the tarn and are the highest greenslate quarries in the country. It is quite possible that they would have been in operation in the 1600s or even before. But the first records that we have are from 1792 when John Wilson conducted his survey of the slate industry for Lady le Fleming. He reported that the quarries, which were then called Highwater Quarries, were worked by three men and had been 'rubbished up' following an accident. However the quality of the product was 'superfine' and the quarry had excellent prospects so long as it had good management. Three years later Low Water was to change hands. In a lease dated 13 February 1795 Sir Michael

142

le Fleming let the workings to Messrs Jackson, Knott and Harrison for an annual rent of £10. The royalties paid were 3/- a ton for best slate and the new proprietors had to employ, at all times, at least *"ten fit and proper workmen to work the quarries."* In those days made-slates were carried down by pack pony.

During the period 1850 to 1930 the quarries were under the Mandall's umbrella and were worked more or less continuously by no more than one company of men making a small but significant contribution to the output of Mandall's Old Man quarries. Three men working during the 1920s were Harold Grisedale, Melly Dixon snr. and Jack Tarr. Low Water was a dark and sombre place, especially in winter when the quarry would not see the sun until well into April. If the weather was fine the men would 'walk out onto the end' to get some sun while they ate their bait. As well as working Low Water the group were also responsible for opening a small working nearby on the north east shoulder of Coniston Old Man. A short level was taken in and a small closehead opened up. The three always maintained that they were being asked to drive the level too high. They felt it should have been driven about 80ft lower down. They were clearly right. The level skimmed the top of the band. Little slate was obtained and the workings were soon abandoned.

The old cart track constructed by Mandalls up to Low Water Quarry now serves as part of the climbers' track to the summit of the mountain. Remains of the former pony track can be made out running more or less parallel to and slightly higher than the cart track.

Those unfamiliar with the area might be excused for walking right past the quarries without seeing them. Falls of natural scree from above have obliterated the cuttings to the levels and the spoil heaps have mellowed so well that they now look as if they are natural features. A low and a high level runs into the hillside. It is not known whether the closeheads join up inside. During the winter of 1995 industrial archaeologists investigated the entrances. Debris was cleared from above the site of the bottom level and eventually one person was able to lower himself into the level mouth. He could see that the first section of the level had been supported by timber head-trees. It was quite evident to him that they had all collapsed for a considerable distance and the tunnel was choked by debris falling in from above. He removed himself quickly from the dangerous position he was in and the excavations were carefully returned to their previous state. It is very unlikely that anyone will ever again be able to walk into these closeheads just beneath the summit of the mountain.

Out on the quarry bank there are the remains of two cabins and a riving shed. The highest working of all is slightly above and to the east of the main quarries, more or less on the shoulder of the mountain. All that remains now is a cutting into which much debris has fallen.

143

On a stormy day with low cloud, high winds and driving rain it is inconceivable to think that men could ever climb up to this remote spot each day to work. As if to prove that they did, on a rock face in the lowest cutting, five names and initials have been carved by chisel. They can still be deciphered and are:

'W. Gregg 1898; J. D. and I. R.; John Hellen and Jo Hellen August 9 1898'

QUARRIES IN COPPERMINES VALLEY

As well as the rich veins of copper, both the silver-grey and light green slate bands pass through the Coppermines Valley. Little silver-grey slate had been worked until Low Brandy Crag Quarry was re-opened in 1982. Slate has been extracted in the valley for many years from the light green band.

Low Brandy Crag
SD284983

Prior to commencing open-top operations in 1982, slate workings at Low Brandy Crag consisted only of three small underground quarries and a tiny surface working. It was in the 1870s that the Mandall Company started to carry out trials in this area and drove the levels to try and intersect the silver-grey band. The venture was not very successful and the trials were not developed to any extent. However, during the next twenty years these small quarries were worked from time to time and contributed a few tons to the total output from Mandall's workings and featured in the royalty returns to the le Fleming Estates. After 1914 no work at all was done until Burlington Slate embarked on their project 75 years later to develop Low Brandy Crag as a modern operation to provide them with a source of silver-grey slate.

Lad Stone End slate workings
SD288991

In 1792 John Wilson reported to Lady le Fleming that 'Ladstone' Quarry had "*very good prospects*" and contained "*a large quantity of slate metal.*" Unfortunately his enthusiasm was never realised. Quarrying here was not progressed because it was feared it would interfere with the expansion of the copper workings on the nearby Bonsor Vein. It was only after the mining activity ceased that the Coniston Mining Syndicate worked it for a few months, paying a royalty of 18/- to the estate for their trouble.

It was in 1909 that a level was driven at a lower point than the original workings and a small amount of slate was obtained. Within five years all activity had ceased.

Lad Stone End workings are located at the entrance to the hanging valley of Red Dell (which, the author is informed, is derived from the old name of

'Riddle'). The lowest workings lie just above the track close to the wooden footbridge over Red Dell Beck. A small dressing shed has been modified in recent years into a lean-to shelter. The level runs in from a cutting at the back of the bank for about 90ft to a small closehead. It is interesting to note that rid from the workings has over-run the water-race which once carried water to the Old Engine Shaft wheel, confirming that the quarry was worked after the wheel was abandoned.

Higher up the fell the spoil from the much older workings can be seen. The silver-grey slate band outcrops here and has been worked in at least four locations on the crag. This area would benefit from a careful study by industrial archaeologists. All aspects point to it being one of the earliest slate workings at Coniston. At the largest working there is evidence of several hand-bored shot holes and remains of two small cabins. The working face here appears to contain significant quantities of good slate which it might be possible to exploit in the future.

SLATE WORKINGS WITHIN THE COPPERMINES

In at least two locations slate from the silver-grey band has been worked within the Coniston Copper Mine itself. This occurred towards the end of the life of the mine and was probably done in a desperate attempt to maintain some revenue. The two locations known to the writer, in Taylor's Level and Deep Level, will be described briefly.

Taylor's Level was driven during the early years of the 19th Century. The level was commenced from a point mid-way between the Coppermines Valley and Red Dell and was driven in a northerly direction towards the Bonsor copper vein. After about 150ft the level intersected and passed through part of the silver-grey slate band. In about 1908 slate from here was worked as a tiny closehead for about twelve months producing a small quantity of roofing slate which was reputed to be of a very high quality. Why the venture was not developed in a bigger way is uncertain.

Some years ago the Coppermines historian, the late Eric Holland, unblocked the entrance to Taylor's Level and waded up it to the closehead where he found a fine iron jumper drill. Since then the level has been more or less accessible but, because of the depth of water, a visit to the closehead cannot be recommended.

A few years ago the author, along with colleagues from Cumbria Amenity Trust, abseiled down through the ancient stopes into the easterly extension of Deep Level from a point on the fellside above the Red Dell track. Here they found the remains of the slate workings of the 1890s which, during a four year period, produced over 150 tons of slate. In fact for a six month period in 1895 the Coniston Mining Syndicate paid the Estate royalties of £6.4s.6d for slate compared to 9s for

145

copper ore, suggesting the major product from the Coniston Copper Mines during this period was, in fact, slate!

At this time access to this area was relatively easy via Deep Level adit. However, today, the easterly extension of Deep Level is completely blocked by collapses and now the only way to the underground slate working is by the method described.

Blue Quarries
SD293985-295987

Blue Quarries lie up the hillside behind the terrace of cottages known as Miner's Row. The quarries work the light green slate band.

Prior to 1860 there is little detail available of the operation of Blue Quarry. We know that, by this date, both the upper and lower quarry were well established. It is very likely, therefore, that the workings would have existed in the late 1790s, and yet the quarries are not mentioned in John Wilson's survey of 1792. There is also no mention in the le Fleming archives of Blue Quarry from this time even though it must have been providing valuable royalties for the Lords of the Manor. The answer to this puzzle may be quite simple. Both Wilson's survey and the manorial records refer to 'Abovebeck Quarries' which, by a process of elimination, are most likely to be Blue Quarries. No doubt further research in the archival records will confirm this.

Wilson refers to Abovebeck Quarries as being in '*good condition*' which, '*if properly managed, would turn to good account*'. However the slate produced was rather hard. In 1841 the lease to Blue Quarry was taken up by the Mandall Company, and, effectively, remained with them and their successors until Blue Quarry closed in 1939.

Slate from Blue Quarry was always difficult to rive. Mandalls experienced problems with the operation and nearly disposed of the lease in 1904. Quite a few other operators were ready to grab it if they had done so but, in the end, the Company held on to Blue Quarry and persevered with trying to make the operation pay.

Blue Quarry is normally considered as being in three sections. Low Blue was worked from a level which has been completely run in. Middle Blue was an open pit working, as was High Blue.

The main route of access to Blue Quarry is from the unsurfaced road that serves Miner's Row. The road runs over the lowest spoil bank passing, on the right, the collapsed bottom level of Low Blue Quarry out of which most of the contents of the lowest bank was brought. The access route climbs up on the left hand side of the spoil bank and then doubles back onto the top. A cutting from the top of the bank appears to have served a level which is now completely blocked by rid tipped from above. From this bank the track continues towards Middle Blue.

On the bank of Middle Blue Quarry are the remains of a small riving shed behind which is the open pit. The floor of the quarry rises steeply. Access into the pit is hazardous but possible higher on the north side for those who are competent scramblers. From the lowest part of the pit a shaft descends into the workings of Low Blue. Many years ago the author descended the shaft by abseiling down a single rope. The shaft is vertical for about fifty feet and then inclines at an easy angle for another 30ft. At the bottom of the descent the Low Blue level contained about 4ft of extremely cold water. There was no means of exit other than by prusicking back up the rope to Middle Blue.

A considerable amount of debris has fallen into the quarry pit which must have changed considerably since it was last worked by quarrymen in 1939. At the top the quarry pit runs into a closehead.

The track from Middle Blue to High Blue runs across the top of the Middle Blue pit. Much of the width of the track has already fallen away into the bottom of the lower quarry. The last section of the road into High Blue is extremely well paved and is obviously designed for horses and carts. At the top of the road is a completely intact riving shed, one of the few remaining intact ones in the district and nearby is a ruined bait cabin. Just behind a level formerly ran into the hill.

On a higher bank are the remains of the anchors and pier for the aerial flight. This was constructed by the Mandall Company during the 1920s to carry slate clog from High Blue to the Coppermines Valley for processing. All that remains now is the slate pillar complete with steps. From the top of the steps the operator could watch the descent of the laden cradle of slate to the valley. Towards the back of the bank is a derelict bait cabin above which, still in place in the crag, are the massive bars which acted as anchors for the aerial flight cables. Access into the quarry pit is easy. It is quite clear that the walls of the pit are extremely unstable and massive sections of rock have fallen away since High Blue was last worked in 1939.

There still appears to be good slate present in all three sections of Blue Quarries. Whether the slate possesses good bate, or whether it would be economic to extract it for architectural use is another question.

Two further small workings in the vicinity of the Coppermines Valley will be mentioned briefly. Towards the bottom of a high ravine, directly opposite Mines House (the cottage owned by the Barrow Mountaineering Club), is a small working that became known as 'Old Man Old Wife Quarry' (SD292988). The quarry is on very steep ground and most of the slate extracted was from a level driven into an isolated pocket of silver grey slate. The quarry is said to have got its name from the fact that it was operated by an elderly couple who rode to work on a donkey.

A steep scramble up from Old Man Old Wife Quarry brings one to the path from the Coppermines to Tilberthwaite. This is a very popular walker's route to

147

and from Wetherlam, as well as a route over to the Tilberthwaite valley. The track passes through the narrow defile known locally as Hole Rake and then descends towards the marshy depression of Crook Moss. On the high, undulating fell, to the right of the track, will be found the scattered workings of Moor Quarry (SD296994). These workings, also on the silver grey band, made a useful contribution to Mandall's output during the 1890s. All that remains now are a few open works, one of which runs into a small, flooded chamber, and a dressing shed with distant views over the Howgill Fells and Yorkshire Dales.

TILBERTHWAITE QUARRIES

Goats Crag Quarry
NY308002

These old and little known workings are situated on the face of Yewdale Crags above the lower part of the Tilberthwaite Valley. There is scant information available of the earliest years of operation but the workings are marked on the 1860 maps and by 1880 had become quite important. In 1924 the lease was taken up by Mr Bennett Johns after he had retired from Honister Quarries. Although he was well into old age, the slate industry was still in his blood and, with a handful of local men, he worked the light green slate of Goats Crag in a traditional manner for a few years until it became impossible to continue. Since then the lease to Goats Crag has not been taken up by anyone else.

Approximately 100 yards beyond the cattle grid, on the road leading to High Tilberthwaite, the old peat track leaves the valley and climbs the hillside before swinging back in a southerly direction towards the peat mosses beyond the top of Yewdale Crags. The lower part of this peat road was used for access to the quarry workings and the quarry track branches off after about 200 yards.

The quarry track, although steep, has obviously been improved by Bennett Johns and is extremely well constructed. For part of the length it is covered with dressing-waste suggesting that sledges might have been used on it at one time. At the top of the track are the ruins of a riving shed and other buildings and a short distance above is another collection of substantial buildings, one of which could have been a stables. Ahead is the main open-top quarry into which a considerable quantity of debris has fallen since the workings closed. On the upper bank is a further dressing shed with a small cabin attached and high on the north side of the quarry is a further shed with signs of a track leading to it.

The fact that there are dressing sheds and spoil tips at various horizons suggests that the quarry was worked as a classic terrace operation for a period of time. There are no suggestions in old maps that Goats Crag was ever worked by closehead although there is always the chance that one of the lease holders may have driven a level along the slate band at some time.

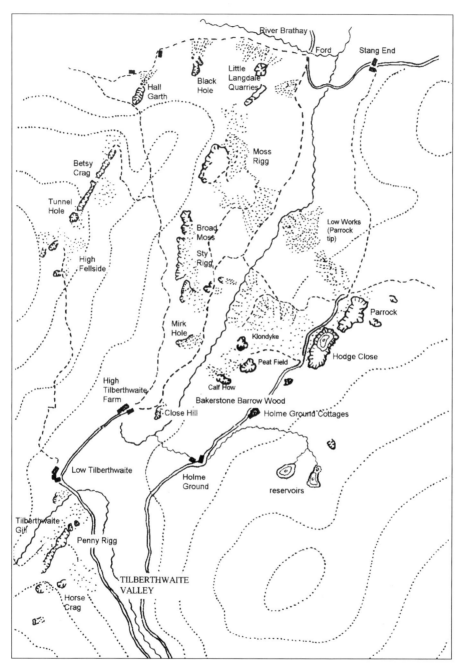

Sketch map showing the slate workings in the Tilberthwaite area

149

Penny Rigg Quarries
NY305008

These ancient workings on the silver-grey band extend up the shoulder of the fell above Low Tilberthwaite for about 500ft and are very evident from the valley road. They lie just to the south and parallel to Tilberthwaite Gill and the spoil from the workings cascades down into the gill. The quarry has had an interesting history and is one of the earliest to have been developed. By 1750 the Lords of the Manor were receiving a considerable amount of revenue from Penny Rigg. In January 1752 a stock-take at the quarry produced a figure of 600 tons valued at over £37 which were held on the quarry bank. During this period, slate was carted from the quarry to the head of Coniston Lake for shipment down to the coast.

In 1825 the quarry featured in the account of Mr J Corry in his *History of Lancashire*. He refers to the fact that "*at Penny Rigg Quarry the slate is conveyed on trucks through a level drain into the side of the rock, at some height above the bottom of the pit.*" This feature can still be seen today.

The bottom of the main bank has today been cleared to provide a car park for those visiting Tilberthwaite Gill or climbing Wetherlam. The cart road to the quarry left the valley road at the top of the rise just to the south of the car park. On the flat top of the lowest tip are the remains of a building, possibly a riving shed and at the back of the bank a level formerly ran into a closehead. This is now completely blocked. Two more small levels ran off the track to the left (south). The upper of the two is still open and leads to a small closehead. Further up, also on the left, a cutting leads into the base of the main Penny Rigg quarry. This is assumed to be the feature referred to by Mr Corry as being the '*level drain*' in the side of the rock through which slate was carried from the base of the pit. A rock fall on the far (south) wall which occurred in 1994 shows the unstable nature of the rock in these open-top quarries.

In the lowest point of the pit, on the far left, the upper entrance to the tunnel referred to as the Quarry Adit is now completely blocked. It was during the 1870s that the Quarry Adit was driven to supply water to the water-wheel at the Horse Crag copper workings further down the valley. The Penny Rigg quarry pit was flooded to act as a reservoir and one must assume that little slate working took place at this time. However by 1892 the quarries were again back in operation having been re-opened by Thomas Warsop, inventor and mining engineer. Final closure appears to have been sometime in the 1930s when the Shaw family were the proprietors.

From this lowest point the base of the pit rises in a succession of terraces. On the left side a considerable quantity of rid has been tipped from above. Remains of a dressing shed are on the floor of the pit. At the higher terrace are the remains of a substantial riving shed and just behind, on the rock face, two slots in

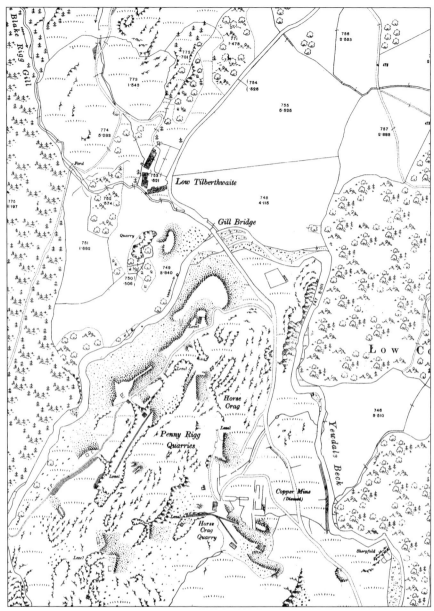

This section of the 1915 edition of the Ordnance Survey shows the Penny Rigg area in Tilberthwaite. At first sight little appears to have changed over the years but on closer inspection a number of levels are marked which are now over-run with spoil and, to the left, the larch plantation of Blake Rigg, planted to provide timber for the mines, has now been almost completely cleared.

The Penny Rigg pit is marked clearly as is the Horse Crag slate working which was being operated at this time by the Shaw family. Adjacent to Horse Crag the much older copper ore processing site is marked. This handled ore brought out of John Barrett's formidable and very costly Horse Crag Level that ran from here all the way into the depths of the Tilberthwaite Mine – and took ten years to construct.

151

the wall suggest that part of a wooden structure was located here, possibly a lifting derrick. From here carts carrying slates could leave the quarry through a wide cutting to gain access to the track down to the valley road. Just outside are the remains of a well built cabin with mortared walls and a fire-place.

On the top bank an embankment has been constructed across the floor and has, at one time, carried a rail track. It ran from an underground closehead to the riving shed. Today the entrance to the level is extremely precarious and is in imminent danger of collapse. The level itself is completely blocked after about 50ft. On no account should it be entered.

This area was the last worked at Penny Rigg and the method of operation is quite clear. Slate clog would be brought out from the closehead along the tunnel and across the bank to the riving shed where slates would be made and carted away. It is possible to scramble out onto the fellside from the top of Penny Rigg. On the sides of the open pit there is still some good slate rock that could be extracted.

From the top of Penny Rigg it is possible, for those properly equipped, to descend down the fellside to the road at Horse Crag. Just beyond the edge of the quarry is a small underground working. On the bank is a large dressing shed and a cabin. Just below another large dressing shed has been used in more recent times by the local farmer. Below here is the Horse Crag open-top quarry and also the entrance to Horse Crag Level which is currently being worked. On no account should these workings be disturbed.

From the roadside below Horse Crag the more observant will notice the different colours of the material on the nearby spoil tips. On one of the tips, brown waste material (which is, in fact, of copper ore) has been overlaid by slate rid and a brief explanation for the reason for this will be given.

The ruined buildings here are the site of the Penny Rigg Copper Mill. By the 1840s the Tilberthwaite Copper Mine, a quarter of a mile away at the head of the gill, was increasing in size. In 1849 John Barrett approved a major development to drive a long level of some 3200ft. from this point to intersect the mine. The level would provide drainage and allow copper ore to be removed easily. The actual details of this undertaking have been given earlier in the chapter 'Between the Wars'. The copper mill was constructed close to the exit of the long level. During the 1930s, after copper mining ceased, slate was also worked from this level and this accounts for the presence of slate spoil on the banks of copper mine waste.

Water to power the water wheel at the Penny Rigg Copper Mill was provided by building a take-off point above the first waterfall in Tilberthwaite Gill and constructing a water leat to convey water along the side of the gill and over the shoulder of the fell to the mill.

From High Tilberthwaite the spoil tips of the Penny Rigg slate workings can be seen cascading down towards the bed of Tilberthwaite Gill. Penny Rigg worked the silver-grey slate band by a mixture of underground closeheads and an open pit. The closeheads became quite sizeable but the entrances to them all are now completely blocked.   *Photo – A Cameron*

153

As Penny Rigg Quarry increased in size it eventually severed the line of the water leat and a new leat was constructed which was much higher and took water from Crook Beck some distance away. Whether compensation was agreed between the two parties or whether the lease holders of the quarry paid for the construction of the new water system is not known, although there are stories locally that relationships between the two could have been better.

For a number of years, while the quarry was not being worked, water from the leat was diverted and allowed to pour into the quarry to form a reservoir. A tunnel was driven from the base of the quarry pit to the Penny Rigg Mill and for a period of time water was provided this way.

Close Hill Quarry
NY309014

This quarry is adjacent to High Tilberthwaite Farm and worked a branch of the light green band. It is best seen by looking over the wall at the side of the road leading from the farm to Little Langdale ford. The quarry is virtually directly below. An open pit leads to a closehead. Access is over private land and the pit is full of household rubbish thrown from the road above. There are very few references to the workings. However in 1825 it was worked by Messrs Woodburn and Coward and, along with a number of other Tilberthwaite quarries, it was sited on land which was not part of a manor. Consequently all 'royalties' went to the community of Tilberthwaite. A spoil bank extends across the adjoining field and there are few remains of interest.

Mirk Hole Quarry
NY311018

Further along the road to the Little Langdale ford the Low Mirk Hole workings are the first to be reached. Judging from the appearance of the remains it must date from the mid 18th Century. A series of spoil banks in scrub woodland on the left (west) side of the road are derived from closehead workings. One of the levels has been dammed to provide a source of water. The level at the end has been opened out to form a pit working which shows quite clearly the steep bedding plane of the slate. Slightly higher is a small working on the bank of which is a building which may have been a stable and nearby is a small dressing shed which would not have held more than two people. The most interesting remains here are, however, the traces of a completely circular building with a tree growing out of the middle at the top end of the workings. The walls are very thick and the writer has not been able to find any details about it or what it was used for.

The main Mirk Hole workings are just to the north, beyond the boundary wall. There are two quite large quarry banks covered in scrub birch. The upper one

154

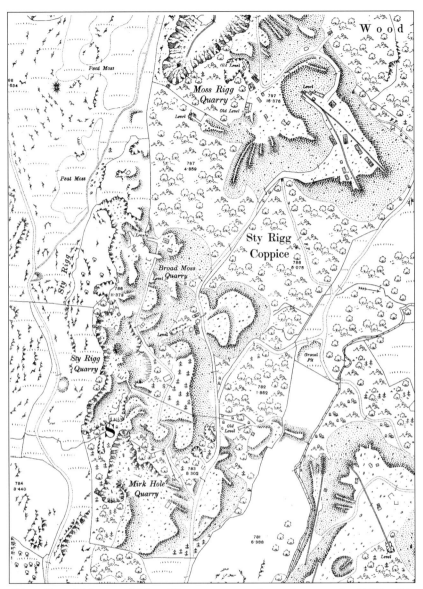

The Sty Rigg, Broad Moss and Moss Rigg areas are shown here on the 1915 edition of the Ordnance Survey. This is a complex collection of old workings on the western slopes of the Tilberthwaite Valley which, at this time, were being operated by the Buttermere Green Slate Company under the watchful eye of their director Bennett Johns. The Company were soon to take over Moss Rigg as well, part of which is shown at the top of the map. The Mirk Hole Quarry towards the bottom was largely worked out at the century's turn.

A number of important levels are marked on this map almost all of which are now over-run with spoil from more recent working. There is certainly the opportunity for industrial historians to re-open several of them, possibly to reveal underground sites which are exactly as they were left when slate extraction ceased. It may also be possible to start present day slate extraction here, in a small way, as there are excellent reserves remaining of rock with good bate and vehicle access is good.

155

covers part of the lower and could have over-run a level in from the lower bank. The northern end of Mirk Hole is adjacent to the Sty Rigg workings.

Sty Rigg and Broad Moss Quarries
NY311020-311022

These are the next quarries reached along the road towards Little Langdale. Although in earlier times they were separate undertakings working the light green slate band, by 1900 they had become one. Sty Rigg must have been worked over a long period of time, perhaps as long as 100 years. Early workings have been over-run by more recent operations. The site is extremely difficult to interpret. At one time a considerable length of narrow gauge rail track was in use linking the faces with the dressing areas. A well graded cart track runs from the valley road into the workings. On the quarry banks at Broad Moss are the remains of a number of buildings. The lowest bank, on the right of the track has been over-tipped with rid from more recent workings. Several levels serving underground chambers are now run-in and blocked. All the most recent working has been on the open faces, some of which now overhang the floors. The quarry was worked right up to the fence line but not beyond, presumably because of restrictions on the lease. A considerable quantity of farm and domestic waste including an old van has been tipped into one area of the quarry. Broad Moss was once operated around 1895 by Mr Bennett Johns, the capable and energetic mining engineer from Ulverston, who subsequently became associated with the Buttermere Green Slate Company. In fact Broad Moss continued to be operated by the Buttermere Company until about 1925. Earlier, in 1825, Sty Rigg was being worked by Messrs Woodburn and Coward and was one of the quarries which provided a royalty for 'the township of Tilberthwaite'.

The most interesting thing about both quarries is that there appears to be good slate still present on the abandoned working faces. There is also good road access. Anyone considering starting a small enterprise to extract and work slate could do a lot worse than consider Broad Moss as a site to do so.

Moss Rigg Quarry
NY313023

Moss Rigg has had a long and interesting history. As with all quarries in the area it worked slate from the light green band although, in fact, the actual slate colour here was predominantly olive green. The quarry started as a series of underground closeheads accessed by one main level and a number of higher subsidiary levels which were abandoned relatively early. The earliest dates of working are not known although it is very likely to have been before 1700. By 1825 Messrs Woodburn and Coward were actively operating the quarry and by 1850 it had become one of the largest in the Tilberthwaite Valley. One of the

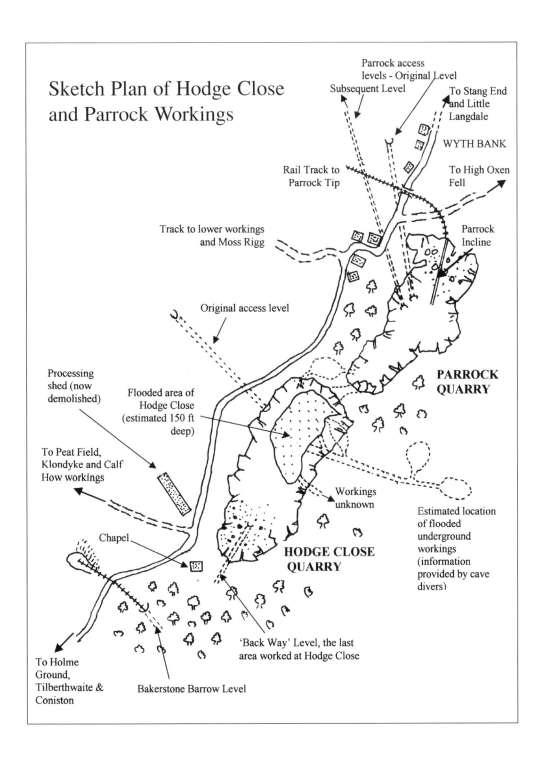

Sketch Plan of Hodge Close and Parrock Workings

Parrock access levels - Original Level

Subsequent Level

To Stang End and Little Langdale

WYTH BANK

Rail Track to Parrock Tip

To High Oxen Fell

Track to lower workings and Moss Rigg

Parrock Incline

Original access level

Processing shed (now demolished)

Flooded area of Hodge Close (estimated 150 ft deep)

PARROCK QUARRY

To Peat Field, Klondyke and Calf How workings

Chapel

Workings unknown

Estimated location of flooded underground workings (information provided by cave divers)

HODGE CLOSE QUARRY

To Holme Ground, Tilberthwaite & Coniston

Bakerstone Barrow Level

'Back Way' Level, the last area worked at Hodge Close

157

chambers had become extremely large and during the 1880s a start was made to convert it to open-top by removing the roof. This had disadvantages. It was an extremely hazardous operation and, once the closehead had been converted to an open pit, the walls were never as secure as before. Rock falls from them were frequent and injuries to the men a fact of life. During the 1890s the quarry was being worked by Messrs Stephenson's Tilberthwaite Green Slate Company along with Hodge Close. The manager was Mr J Thomas. The Company operated Moss Rigg through the Great War but eventually abandoned it early in the 1920s. The lease was then taken up by the Buttermere Company but little work was done by them. Although there was abundant slate present it was hard and difficult to rive.

In 1948, after a further 20 years of not being worked, the lease was taken up by the Lakeland Green Slate and Stone Company. The exploits of this Company are documented in other chapters. The Company worked both the open quarry and the underground closeheads energetically for a further 14 years after which time Moss Rigg has only worked intermittently.

The quarry is entirely on private property and, although not currently worked, the lease is still held by Burlington Slate. Consequently exploration is not recommended. The road up to Moss Rigg passes through a gate and ascends to the top of the extensive quarry bank. Remains of machinery are all around. The main processing sheds are to the left. The oldest buildings here were brought over from Coniston Copper Mines in 1958 and re-built. The former access tunnel to the open pit and closeheads is now completely blocked but was in use until the new road system was constructed from the main bank up to the lip of the quarry pit and then steeply down the south and the west side to the quarry floor. Many of the older workings have been obliterated by the recent operations and construction of the road but to the north of the pit there are traces of a number of old riving sheds and, in the woods, are the remains of a well preserved powder magazine. Because the Lakeland Company experienced severe restrictions on tipping, a quite extensive road system has been constructed from the quarry site running to the north to allow tipping away from the valley. Much of the area of Moss Rigg is rapidly being covered by a blanket of birch, showing that even recent quarry activities can be covered quickly by vegetation.

Hodge Close Quarries
NY316017

These workings in the woods above Holme Ground have had a long and chequered history. They are situated on the Buccleuch Estate, a vast and wealthy estate owned by the Scottish Dukes of Buccleuch and Queensbury. Hodge Close probably started in the late 1780s and continued to be worked, with a few brief periods of inactivity, until 1964.

Interpretation of the site is very difficult because of the vast amount of work done during the 20th Century. Most of the slate has been taken from an offshoot of the light green band. Because the bedding plane is nearly vertical at this point the slate has been worked to a great depth as a pit working. It has always been assumed that the pit was once a closehead from which the roof was removed at some point but archive records tend to suggest that, although this was done at nearby Parrock Quarry, this may not have been the case at Hodge Close.

The road up to Hodge Close is now surfaced as far as the quarry. It passes Holme Ground cottages, built for quarry workers in the 1880s, before descending through the trees to the quarry. On the left is a vast expanse of spoil. During the later years of operation a corrugated steel building was sited here and was the main processing shed for slate manufacture. After closure this survived for a number of years but became damaged by the weather and was removed. Before the Second World War, slates were manufactured in a number of riving sheds in the same area.

On the right hand side of the road is the main quarry pit which is well over 300ft deep. The depth of the workings below the water level is at least equal to that above. A level gains access to the quarry from the lower ground to the west and is still open. Over the years at least three systems were used to lift slate clog from the depths out of the quarry. In the final years of the 19th Century a water balance lift raised slate up to the access level from where it was taken out to be processed in riving sheds on the lower banks. For a period of time a steam crane was used until it became damaged by a fall of rock.

During the 20th Century a blondin crane was installed running across the width of the pit from the north west to south east. More recently the blondin was re-aligned to run from south to north and was used right up to closure of the quarry. Remains of the supports for the blondin can be found on the quarry rim. It is said locally (no doubt with exaggeration) that Hodge Close closed because the Company could not afford a new blondin rope.

Just to the right of the road as it descends from the wood is the location of the Bakerstone Barrow Level, one of the last areas to be worked. The author can remember the rail track crossing the road to the spoil bank on the other side. Just below, also on the right, are the remains of the old chapel and community centre. This was in use within living memory for social events and for services once a month. Sadly the building has been badly vandalised. Adjacent to the chapel are the remains of the smithy which, well within living memory, was intact. It even had the old bellows in place. Behind the chapel are traces of an old lagoon and, nearby, the bed of the support for the blondin crane. When the water balance lift was in operation water to fill the balance tank was taken by pipe from a reservoir higher up the fellside. The pipe ran past the chapel and along the side of the pit to the top of the lift.

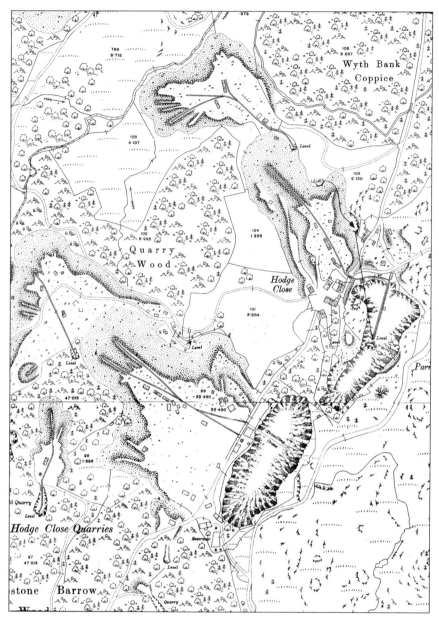

Ninety years ago the Hodge Close and Parrock Quarries were already very extensive. At Hodge Close the blondin crane was still in its old position across the width of the pit with rail tracks from the blondin landing leading across the main bank. At Parrock the incline is in place. From the top of the incline a rail track crosses the road by a bridge and runs onto the over-tip spoil heap, developed to avoid incurring high land rent costs from tipping further out over the valley.

The original spoil from Hodge Close was removed by a long access tunnel and tipped across the former woodland, almost encroaching in places into Pierce How Beck. Subsequently this area was also over-tipped by spoil removed from the Hodge Close quarry by the blondin crane. The map also shows part of the large number of smaller workings in Bakerstone Barrow Wood.

160

From close to the chapel a series of ladders once descended the sides of the quarry pit and were used for access in the final years of operation. At the bottom of the quarry a level ran in to the south and was known as 'Back Way'. This area has recently been much altered by tipping into the pit from nearby quarrying operations which are still going on. At the far (north) end of the quarry is the archway through to the Parrock Quarry. To the left of the archway a level can be seen. This enters a flooded closehead at roof height.

It is possible to walk right round the top of Hodge Close pit, with care. At a number of points the remains of the various hoisting arrangements of former years can be seen including the blondin anchors and the water pipe which once supplied water to the water balance lift.

Close to the collection of buildings and cottages a rough road runs down towards the bottom of the valley. After a short distance it passes the exit of the access level into the Hodge Close pit. When the water balance lift was in operation much of the product from the quarry would have been brought out of here. It is possible to walk along the tunnel for those properly equipped although the water level is up to knee-height. A few meters further on the road forks. The left hand fork leads to the lower bank.

The lower bank has been much altered by more recent tipping above. To the right the fingers of spoil stretch out over the valley. At least two levels ran in from the left. Both were accessible until recently, one was nearly 300 yards long and ended at a blind forehead. At the far end of the lower bank two levels are still accessible and lead to a series of small chambers deep beneath Bakerstone Barrow Wood.

By climbing up into the trees from the furthest extent of the lower bank, the keen explorer will find himself at the end of the bed of a mineral line which was known locally as Calf How Cutting. This leads through the woods to the Calf How workings. Much of the route of the line remains intact. The Calf How Quarries worked the light green slate band by closehead and open pits.

Hodge Close has found a new use in recent years for outdoor pursuits. A large number of climbing routes have been put up on the sides of the quarry, especially around the arch and on the slabs on the east side. Unfortunately the climbers are hampered by the fact that large areas of the rock face become detached from time to time and disappear into the depths below. The flooded pit and a number of deep chambers off it are also popular with sub-aqua divers. Because of the popularity of the quarry, especially at weekends, the planning authorities are becoming worried about the level of use and local residents are concerned about privacy.

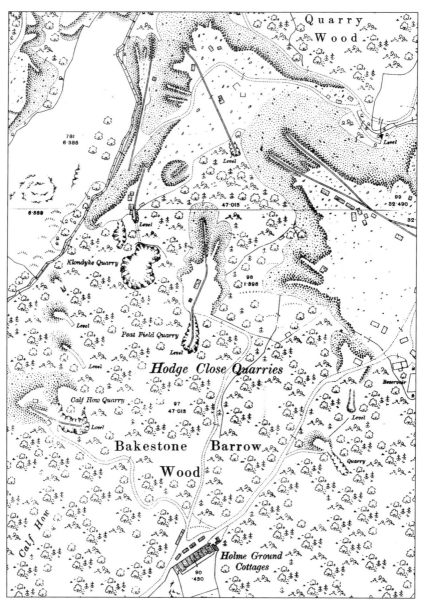

Within Bakerstone Barrow Wood at Holme Ground quite a number of slate workings were started in the second half of the 19th Century. Most were worked by the Buttermere Company on and off until the start of the Second World War. In 1987 Sam Dugdale re-opened the Peat Field working which was taken over nine years later by Billy Gibson and Martin Askew of Coniston. More recently Peat Field has been sold to Burlington Slate who are, at the time of writing, actively developing the site.

Most of the abandoned remains that exist today are shown on this 1915 map, with the exception of the rail line between the Klondyke workings and Calf How quarries which was constructed after the Great War.

In 1915 the inhabitants of Holme Ground Cottages were quarrymen and their families. Sadly most of the cottages are now 'second-homes'.

162

Parrock Quarry
NY318018

One of the earliest references to Parrock Quarry was in 1866 when the lease was taken up by John Nevison of Langdale from the Buccleuch Estates. At this time the quarry was entirely an underground operation. By 1897 Parrock had been taken over by the Buttermere Green Slate Company along with a number of other workings nearby. The following year an extremely serious accident occurred at Parrock. The roof to the largest underground closehead was being removed, an operation which was known locally as 'open-topping'. A Cornishman by the name of John Bond was working on the face when he was covered by a very large quantity of rock that had fallen from the half removed roof. It took five weeks to locate his body during which time no working for slate took place. Rescue operations were frequently hampered by the constant stream of sightseers watching from the rim of the quarry.

Parrock continued to be operated by the Buttermere Company until about 1930.

During the most recent operation, slate was removed from the pit via an incline at the northern end. Exactly how this incline operated is uncertain. Prior to the incline being commissioned all slate was taken out along the access levels. Two long levels served the quarry while it was being worked as an underground operation. A level of about 300 yards ran in from the lowest bank. About 280 yards is accessible today, the remainder is completely blocked by collapsed roof timbers. A higher level running in from below the cottages opened out close to the incline foot.

A considerable amount of slate was removed from the lower level, as can be seen by the extensive spoil bank stretching across the valley. As well as serving the main Parrock pit the level also allowed the working of quite a number of closeheads reached by branch tunnels running off the main drive.

Betsy Crag and Tunnel Hole Quarries
NY307025-306022

These workings on the silver-grey band are located at the base of the east face of Wetherlam. The cart track to the quarries leaves the rough road from High Tilberthwaite to Hall Garth (Little Langdale) near its highest point and swings across marshy ground to the lowest part of the Betsy Crag workings. Just past the gate, at the foot of the spoil bank, a substantial level will be seen. This goes in for some 60ft. to a walled up bank. The level then swings left through a short length of Mat Spedding tunnelling to end at a tiny closehead which has been worked upwards for a short way prior to being abandoned. This was obviously an attempt to work the silver grey band at a lower depth. It is possible that they intended to drive the working upwards to come up beneath the main Betsy Crag quarry above.

Outside the entrance are the remains of a small riving shed and, just below the track, a round cabin with a narrow entrance. Close to the gate are also the remains of what appears to have been a loading wharf.

The cart road runs up to the top of the bank. Here are the remains of some buildings and stacks of slate. Some of the buildings have been altered considerably. Beyond is the edge of the main Betsy Crag pit-working. There is a dressing shed in the base of the pit but the method used to get the slate from here to the top is uncertain. Above is a long narrow tip which is associated with the higher Betsy Crag quarry which is much older.

On the floor of the higher quarry are the remains of a substantial building which could have been a stable. From behind the building a former track can be traced rising steeply to the rim of the quarry through which it passes via a narrow cleft. The track then descends the fellside beyond on a slightly raised causeway. This was most likely once the route for carts to and from the upper working.

To the west of Betsy Crag, above the quarry rim, are excellent examples of glaciation marks and clearly defined bedding planes, which should be of interest to geologists.

Higher up the fellside the Tunnel Hole workings are extremely interesting. There is an assortment of old buildings, one of which may have been for accommodation. Some of the walling of the structures is very fine.

Between Tunnel Hole and Betsy Crag the level which once joined the two workings is now blocked at the Betsy Crag end. However on the Tunnel Hole side the level can be accessed and this short, hidden length of blind tunnel was once one of the sites of an illicit still operated by the infamous Lanty Slee. Lanty worked in the slate and copper industries between the years 1840 to 1880. He had a number of sites in the Tilberthwaite area where he could set up his still and he would frequently move sites to avoid detection. He has become an almost legendary figure in the Coniston area. The writer once gained access to this short length of tunnel, using a rope and noticed that there was still a substantial pile of ash on the floor from the hearth. Beneath a slab in the floor is a hidden 'safe' in which Lanty could hide his equipment.

The higher Tunnel Hole workings are also interesting. At one point a narrow cleft in the side of the pit gives access to the floor. A slab of slate across the top of the cleft acts as a footbridge. The west face of the quarry dangerously overhangs the quarry floor. A lot of work would be required here before this face could be worked safely again. There are the examples of both hand-drilled shot holes on the east face and power-drilled holes on the west. Remains of a substantial dressing shed are on the floor of the pit.

Starting from the end of the quarry bank, just below the slab bridge, are the remains of a well engineered path that traverses the extremely steep hillside towards an extensive spoil tip to the south. This is a quarry man's path which was

This photograph of men and boys at Moss Rigg workings is felt to originate from about 1890 when the site was operated by the Tilberthwaite Green Slate Company. Of interest is the hand sledge holding several hundredweight of slate. The pegs butting from the ends of the shafts helped pull the sledge along.

In about 1901 Moss Rigg was taken over by The Buttermere Green Slate Company and continued operating under their banner until the workings were closed down in the 1930s. In 1948 the workings were opened again by the Lakeland Green Slate and Stone Company.

Photo – Ruskin Museum archives

used to gain access to the working bank on the top of the tip. Here are the remains of a few buildings including dressing sheds and a shelter cabin. From the back of the bank a level runs through solid rock to gain access to the top Tunnel Hole workings.

High on the west rim of Tunnel Hole, in a very exposed location, are the remains of a quite substantial building, with no windows, but a doorway through its extremely thick walls. It may once have been a powder magazine although there does not appear to have been any timber lining to the inside of the walls. Close to here a rock fall, which occurred in the summer of 1995, has exposed what appears to be an area of excellent slate rock.

The top working at Tunnel Hole is a pit which, from above, appears totally inaccessible without the use of ropes and abseil equipment. However a level, which is out of sight from above, runs in from the main bank which is situated on the steep hillside to the east. Access to this bank by the quarry man's path has been described above.

How finished slates were carried from here down to the road below is a mystery. There is a suggestion that a sledge track may have run down the north edge of the tip. At the base of the tip there are quite clearly the remains of a loading wharf and a track leading away. Could hand-sledging have been carried out here in the same way as at Honister? Another suggestion that has been made is that a steep aerial flight may have run down to a point close to the cart road below. Careful investigation is required to confirm.

By the end of the 18th Century these workings were well established and had probably been in operation for at least 50 years previously. During the early years of the 1800s Betsy Crag was being worked by a colourful local character called Solomon Robinson. He originated from Ambleside and took great delight in completely ignoring the wishes of the land owners on whose property he worked. Eventually he abandoned Betsy Crag and went to work the slab quarries in the woods of Brathay. In 1825 the workings were being operated by a Mr Turner who worked Betsy Crag by 'running a level under the hill'. By 1840 both Betsy Crag and Tunnel Hole were extensive, the layout of the workings was not dissimilar to today.

The last working at Tunnel Hole was in the 1930s. Earlier in the 20th Century two fatalities occurred there, to Joe Brockbank and also to Robert Fell. Mr Fell was killed as he returned to inspect a charge that had not gone off. His relatives still live locally.

CONISTON'S FLAG QUARRIES

The band of sedimentary slate passes quite close to Coniston village and has been worked in many places. Virtually all of these workings are on private property. There are hardly any remains of interest within the flag quarries and most are small, damp and dismal workings which are choked with brambles. Consequently the writer cannot recommend that anyone wastes time visiting them and the account that follows is for completion only.

In the intake fields above Outrake and Heathwaite Farms are a number of sites which were referred to generally as the Outrake Quarries. Today they appear to be nothing more than natural rocky outcrops and if it was not for the fact that they are marked on the large scale maps, there would be no indication that these outcrops had once been small flag quarries. In 1885 these workings were being operated by John Bowness who lived at Outrake Farm and who paid a small royalty to the le Fleming Estate for doing so. The writer remembers, as a small boy, being shown a magnificent six foot square slate slab by the farmer at Outrake which was being used to block a hole in an intake wall. He was told that this had come from the nearby flag quarry.

Passing along the line of the sedimentary slate band, the next small workings which are known to have produced flags are situated at the side of the lane leading to Heathwaite Farm. No references to these workings have been found in the archives. Not far from here, above the top terrace of houses at Cat Bank is the Cat Bank Quarry. This was a pit working accessed by a short tunnel. The quarries were worked by the Coniston Slate Company for a number of years and created problems for them as it was very difficult to dispose of waste at such a congested site. Eventually the Company had to purchase six cottages nearby to avoid the owners serving an injunction on them to stop them operating. Cat Bank Quarries worked until the 1920s. Today the pit is overgrown with trees and brambles.

Less than a quarter of a mile to the north are the remains of several flag workings in the gill above the former Coniston railway station. In the Estate records these are collectively known as Coniston Gill Quarries although, no doubt, investigations locally would produce other names. For a while Mr Haimer of the Coniston Slate Company worked these quarries and had constant arguments with the Estate over the dead rent. The workings closed around the time of the First World War and since then the buildings have been converted and enlarged to create a small workshop by the Pickles family. One, Levi Pickles, was an extremely well thought of engineer who was said to be capable of repairing anything! He carried out a lot of work for the Mandalls Company and installed a water wheel in the gill which provided lighting for the workshop buildings.

A few hundred meters further along the slate band some working has taken place in Mealy Gill. Today there are very few remains to show what occurred here but, as with Coniston Gill, this site received the attention of the Coniston Slate Company for a short period in the 1890s. Clearly the demand for slabs must have been falling at this time as no attempt was made to work the slab band at any point other than where slate outcropped, for example, in the beds of the gills. Mealy Gill was also the site of the fledgling Coniston Wad Mine. The lord of the manor, Sir Daniel Fleming, invested in the development of the mine. The only return on his investment was the boot-blacking mill situated at the foot of the gill beside Mines Beck.

Coniston's main slab quarry was in Guards Wood on the high ground between Monk Coniston Hall and Yewdale Valley. Guards Quarry was already extensive by 1850 and had probably been worked for at least sixty years previously. It was still working at the start of the First World War by which time the site was quite extensive.

Today the remains are lost under a mantle of trees. The workings consist of a series of parallel shallow open pits, at least two of which are now flooded. The spoil banks are completely overgrown. The only remains of interest is a magnificent slate built powder magazine which still contains part of the timber lining.

The quarries were situated on land which was part of the Buccleuch Estates. Nearby was Monk Coniston Hall owned by the industrialist Mr Marshall. In September 1884 the estate manager for Monk Coniston, Thomas Everett, was instructed by Mr Marshall to write to the Buccleuch estate office in Dalton asking whether he could purchase the royalties to the quarries. Unfortunately this was not because Mr Marshall was considering becoming a patron of the industry but purely because he was annoyed by the fact that Guards Quarry was becoming an eyesore from his drawing room windows.

A month later Mr Everett wrote to the estate office again suggesting that the reserves of slate were exhausted and the quarry was running at a loss. This must have been refuted by the estate because, on December 4th he wrote a third time qualifying his previous letter somewhat and suggesting that Mr Marshall only wanted to stop slate extraction on the Monk Coniston side of the hill and was prepared to tolerate the working of slate that was out of sight. This was agreed and the quarries continued to work for at least another thirty years.

The woods on the steep hillside behind Monk Coniston Hall were the location of two more slab quarries. That at Monk Coniston Tarn is now completely hidden by woodland. The second location is adjacent to the main Coniston to Hawkshead road and is now used from time to time for the storage of roadstone. The quarry at Monk Coniston Tarn was being worked as long ago as 1720 by the Swainsons and product from here was used for roofing Ulverston church in that year. This is one of the very first references we have to a specific quarry site at Coniston and is interesting because it shows that sedimentary slate from this area could be riven and dressed as roofing slates as well as being made into slabs and flags.

ACKNOWLEDGMENTS and NOTES

Many people were involved in the production of the first edition of this book, a large proportion of whom had direct connections with the industry for the whole of their working lives. Others have had close links with it for one reason or another. During work on the first edition the author was very much indebted to them for the help they were all keen to give. Their names are listed in the Acknowledgments section of that edition. Sadly several have now passed away, but they have left a vital legacy in their stories and descriptions of life and work in Coniston during the earlier decades of the 20th Century. We have now preserved many of these on tape as a developing oral history library.

Since the first edition of *Slate from Coniston* was published research work has continued into the history of this ancient industry and the second edition has included much of this data. The new book also includes a selection of the many extra photographs that have come to life in recent years. When new photographs come to light, they are carefully copied, safely stored in a digital format and the originals returned to their owners. The photographic archive, along with the oral history library, will form a unique collection for future research into Coniston's history.

Work continues to be carried out in the field. Information on this and details on the theories of how we believe the industry started and developed after the Norman Conquest have also been archived. Much of this work has been carried out by a small group of local investigators which has included several who still work in the industry today.

In the acknowledgements of the first edition we mention many individuals and organisations that helped produce that edition. Our thanks to them still stands. Those who have helped with this edition include Donald Kelly of Burlington Slate, Billy Gibson who now also works for Burlington, George Tarr and the retired quarrymen Doug Birkett, Mike Brownlee, Jack Tailforth, Ray Jones and George Hodgson. Mrs Smith of Tilberthwaite Avenue, Coniston, has also provided a considerable amount of information on her husband Burt.

We must also thank local historians Maureen Fleming, Ibby Brown and other members of Coniston's Local History Group who have helped on many occasions with field work and interviews. Coniston's Ruskin Museum has again helped with information and facilities. The Village Archives, housed in the superb library above the museum, has already found itself custodian to the Brownlee Collection of documents – a national collection of material relating to the Lakeland Slate Industry. The Archives may, in the future, find themselves the custodian of the rapidly developing photographic and oral history archive as well.

Since the first edition was published the author has also written *Slate from Honister*, edited *Lakeland's Mining Heritage* and co-written *The Story of Coniston*, all with a strong emphasis on the industrial history of Lakeland communities. Such a study is very incomplete without an understanding of the people and culture of communities involved. At times there is a very fine line to be drawn between Archaeology, Industrial Archaeology and Social History. It is very easy to be side-tracked when studying any of these. But it is essential to maintain a broad view and cover each in a balanced way.

At the time of writing the community of Coniston is under great pressure from many sources. The greatest is from the tourist industry which, although now essential to the community, is frequently seen by Coniston people as turning them into 'beggars in their own land'. The slate industry is clearly essential for creating a balance to tourism and, hopefully, will continue to do so in the future.

GLOSSARY OF TERMS

Many of the terms used in the book, especially those relating to the formation and extraction of slate, are explained within the text. Other terms which may not be specifically covered, or which are used more generally, are defined below.

Aerial flight – system for carrying material via overhead cables.

Bait – quarryman's lunch or break.

Bate – line of cleavage in a block of slate.

Blondin – a system for hoisting material from the base of a quarry using a travelling crane suspended from a cable.

Bargain – an agreement made between a quarry proprietor and a 'Company' of men to extract state from a particular area in an agreed time for an agreed payment.

Cleave (cleavage) – the ability of a piece of slate to split evenly along a particular plane.

Clog – a lump of slate rock, as taken from the quarry face.

Closehead – an underground chamber created by the mining of slate.

Coffin level – a level or tunnel, usually of mediaeval origin, cut so that the cross-section resembles a coffin, thus allowing a man to be able to pass along with the greatest width being at his shoulders.

Company of men – a group of quarrymen, usually between 4 and 6 in number, who negotiated a 'bargain' to quarry slate.

Country rock – rock of no commercial value within which slate is found.

Dressing of slate – the operation of shaping a riven piece to size.

Flag quarries – workings which mainly produced slate flags for flooring.

Forehead – the inner end of a tunnel.

Head tree – a timber framework used for supporting the roof of a tunnel.

Heading blast – a means of detonating a face using explosive packed behind the face.

Level – a tunnel running at a gently inclined angle giving access to inner working areas.

Mat Spedding tunnel – a tunnel with walled sides and roof.

Metal (slate metal) – an alternative term for slate rock.

Mucking out – the clearing of waste on a quarry floor.

Old men – a reference to quarrymen of former generations.

Open-topping – the removal of the roof of an underground closehead.

Overburden – the quantity of material above the area being worked.

Pelton wheel – a form of water turbine.

Pit quarry – a quarry worked as a pit, usually as a result of open-topping.

Powder magazine – a building designed to store explosives.

Rid – waste material. It was also a name given to a group of workers who were responsible for clearing waste from a quarry.

Royalty payments – payments to the land owner for the quantity of slate produced.

Rive – the process of splitting slate rock.

Riving hammer – a traditional tool, now no longer used, for splitting slates.

Riving sheds – open fronted buildings in which slate rock was riven.

Slipe – the junction between slate and non slate rock. It is usually well defined.

Shot holes – holes drilled for the insertion of explosive powder.

Water-balanced lift – a system for raising slate clog from a quarry pit using a container of water as the counterbalance.

Wire sawing – a technique for cutting through rock using an endless abrasive wire.

INDEX

Spout Crag Quarry 71, 73, 86, 89, 90, 92, 100
Stockdale Shales 127
Stubthwaite Moss 56, 60, 61, 136, 137, 142
Sty Rigg 16, 18, 32, 155, 156
Summercove 127, 129
Sun Hotel 42, 45, 98

T

Tarr, George or Jack 74, 92, 93, 101, 143, 169
Taylor's Level 44, 145
Tilberthwaite Copper Mine 18, 65, 152
Tilberthwaite Green Slate Company 32, 50, 94,
        158, 165
Tranearth 11, 15, 23, 25, 36, 38, 41, 47, 109,
        123, 125, 127, 128, 130
Tunnel Hole 163, 164, 166

U

Ulverston Canal 13, 15

W

Wadham, Edward 32, 53
Walna Scar 6, 8, 9, 11, 12, 13, 16, 47, 107, 109,
        130, 133, 135
Warsop, Thomas 44, 48, 150
White Quarry 137
Wilson, John 12, 142, 144, 146
Woodburn and Coward 154, 156

Y

Yew Crag 30, 80